Plant
Development

The Green World

Plant
Development

William G. Hopkins

CHELSEA HOUSE
PUBLISHERS
An imprint of Infobase Publishing

Plant Development

Copyright © 2006 by Infobase Publishing

All rights reserved. No part of this book may be reproduced or utilized in any form or by any means, electronic or mechanical, including photocopying, recording, or by any information storage or retrieval systems, without permission in writing from the publisher. For information contact:

Chelsea House
An imprint of Infobase Publishing
132 West 31st Street
New York NY 10001

Library of Congress Cataloging-in-Publication Data

Hopkins, William G.
   Plant development/William G. Hopkins.
      p. cm. — (The green world)
ISBN 0-7910-8562-7
1. Plants—Development—Juvenile literature. 2. Growth (Plants)—Juvenile literature. I. Title. II. Green world (Philadelphia, Pa.)
QK731.H632 2005
571.8'2—dc22   2005026628

Chelsea House books are available at special discounts when purchased in bulk quantities for businesses, associations, institutions, or sales promotions. Please call our Special Sales Department in New York at (212) 967-8800 or (800) 322-8755.

You can find Chelsea House on the World Wide Web at http://www.chelseahouse.com

Text and cover design by Keith Trego

Printed in the United States of America

Bang 21C 10 9 8 7 6 5 4 3 2 1

This book is printed on acid-free paper.

All links, web addresses, and Internet search terms were checked and verified to be correct at the time of publication. Because of the dynamic nature of the web, some addresses and links may have changed since publication and may no longer be valid.

Table of Contents

Introduction

By William G. Hopkins

"Have you thanked a green plant today?" reads a popular bumper sticker. Indeed, we should thank green plants for providing the food we eat, fiber for the clothing we wear, wood for building our houses, and the oxygen we breathe. Without plants, humans and other animals simply could not exist. Psychologists tell us that plants also provide a sense of well-being and peace of mind, which is why we preserve forested parks in our cities, surround our homes with gardens, and install plants and flowers in our homes and workplaces. Gifts of flowers are the most popular way to acknowledge weddings, funerals, and other events of passage. Gardening is one of the fastest-growing hobbies in North America and the production of ornamental plants contributes billions of dollars annually to the economy.

Human history has been strongly influenced by plants. The rise of agriculture in the Fertile Crescent of Mesopotamia brought previously scattered hunter-gatherers together into villages. Ever since, the availability of land and water for cultivating plants has been a major factor in determining the location of human settlements. World exploration and discovery was driven by the search for herbs and spices. The cultivation of New World crops—sugar, cotton, and tobacco—was responsible for the introduction of slavery to America, the human and social consequences of which are still with us. The push westward by English colonists into the rich lands of the Ohio River Valley in the mid-1700s was driven by the need to increase corn production and was a factor in precipitating the French and Indian War. The Irish Potato Famine in 1847 set in motion a wave of migration, mostly to North America, that would reduce the population of Ireland by half over the next 50 years.

As a young university instructor directing biology tutorials in a classroom that looked out over a wooded area, I would ask each group of students to look out the window and tell me what they saw. More often than not, the question would be met with a blank, questioning look. Plants are so much a part of our environment and the fabric of our everyday lives that they rarely register in our conscious thought. Yet today, faced with disappearing rainforests, exploding population growth, urban sprawl, and concerns about climate change, the productive capacity of global agricultural and forestry ecosystems is put under increasing pressure. Understanding plants is even more essential as we attempt to build a sustainable environment for the future.

THE GREEN WORLD series opens doors to the world of plants. The series describes what plants are, what plants do, and where plants fit into the overall scheme of things. In *Plant Development*, the reader is introduced to patterns of development in plants as they progress through the life cycle from seed to mature plant. We learn how plants grow, how they use hormones and signals from their environment to coordinate their development, and how they can measure time.

1 Beginnings

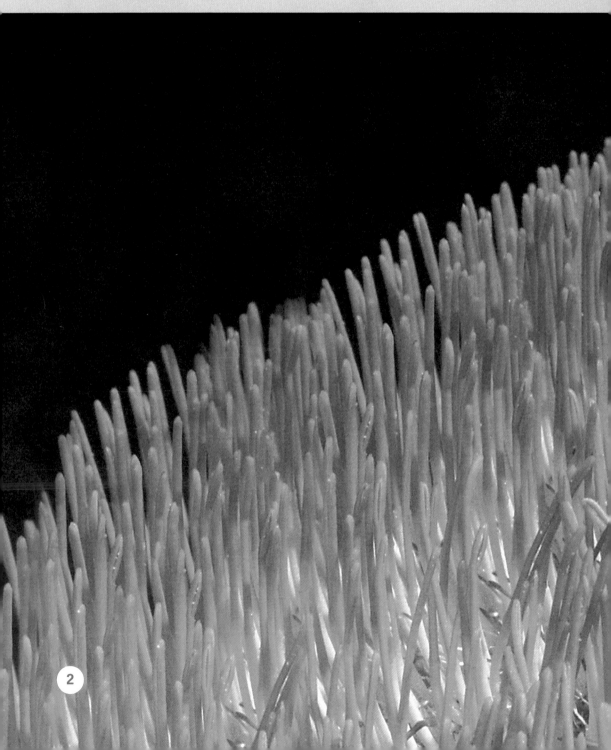

*All the flowers of tomorrow
are in the seeds of yesterday.*

— Proverb

Beginnings

Over 200 years ago, D. Everett wrote the now familiar couplet:

Large streams from little fountains flow
Tall oaks from little acorns grow.

This is the story of how seeds germinate, where new cells come from, and how plants use hormones to direct development. It is the story of how plants detect and use information from their environment, such as light and temperature, and how they use internal clocks to tell time. We will broadly follow the growth and development of plants from seed to seed. In a way, this is the story of how "tall oaks from little acorns grow."

WHAT IS A SEED?

It is sometimes difficult to know where to start when describing a cycle. After all, a cycle by definition has no beginning or end. However, plant life cycles are easier to deal with because of acorns and other seeds. The seed is a convenient place to begin because it represents a natural hiatus in the life cycle of the plant. The dictionary definition of a seed is *the fertilized ovule of a plant and its covering*, but there is a lot more to a seed. A seed is a pretty remarkable structure. A seed contains a miniature plant, or **embryo**, that will develop first into a seedling and then a mature plant of the same kind that it originated from. The embryo is packaged with a store of nutrients that will nourish the seedling as it begins to grow. The whole thing is encased within a protective **seed coat** provided by the maternal plant.

Unlike mature plants that may be 75% or 80% water, mature seeds are very dry. The water content of a seed is typically close to 5%—if an acorn weighs 2 grams, then only 0.1 grams of that is water. Water is essential for vital activities and, because they have so little water, seeds do not respire or show any other obvious signs of life. Some seeds may remain in this state of suspended animation for a very long time. Yet when subjected to appropriate conditions, the embryo will come out of its slumber and renew its growth, the seed will **germinate**, and a new plant will emerge.

In the flowering plants, or **angiosperms**, seeds develop in the **ovary**, the female reproductive structure that is usually located in the center of the flower (Figure 1.1). Seed development follows fertilization of an ovule, or egg, nucleus by the male sperm nucleus delivered to the flower in the form of a pollen grain. Through cell division, the fertilized egg cell, called a **zygote**, gives rise to the embryo. At one end of this embryo is the **plumule**. The plumule is essentially a bud consisting of a growing point or **meristem** surrounded by an undeveloped set of leaves. The plumule is the portion of the embryo that will give rise to the shoot of the plant, including stems, leaves, and flowers. The undeveloped leaves, called the **primary leaves**, will be the first leaves to expand and the first to engage in active photosynthesis when the young seedling emerges from the soil. At the other end of the embryo is the **radicle,** which gives rise to the root system of the plant. Between the plumule and radicle are attached one or more "seed leaves" or **cotyledons.**

The embryos of some flowering plants have only one cotyledon, forming a class known as the **Monocotyledons** (or **monocots**). There are about 65,000 species of monocots including the cereal grains such as wheat, oats, and barley, and other grasses as well as lilies, orchids, and palms. A second class of flowering plants is called the **Dicotyledons** (or **dicots**). Dicots have a pair of cotyledons. There are about 170,000 species of dicots including familiar vegetable crops such as peas and beans, other herbaceous (non-woody) plants, and most trees and shrubs (except for the conifers). The conifers, including the redwoods and pines, are non-flowering plants or **gymnosperms**. Gymnosperms differ from the angiosperms in that the ovules are born naked on cone scales rather than in ovaries as they are in the flowering plants. Otherwise, the seeds of conifers and those produced in flowers

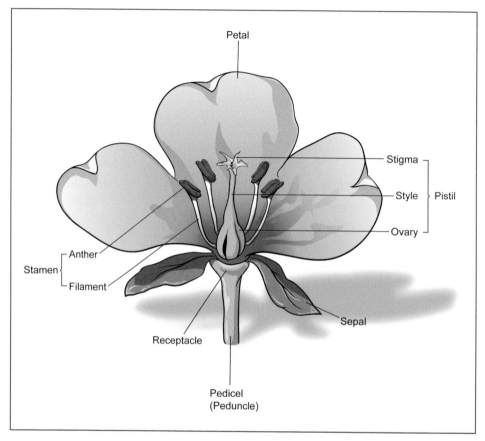

Labels on figure: Petal, Stigma, Style, Pistil, Ovary, Sepal, Anther, Stamen, Filament, Receptacle, Pedicel (Peduncle)

Figure 1.1 The anatomy of a flower includes the stamen, petal, receptacle, pedicel, sepal, and pistil. Seeds develop inside the ovary, the female reproductive structure at the base of the pistil.

are generally similar. The most notable differences are (1) the seeds of the pines, like the ovule, are born naked on the cone scales and (2) the embryo in pine seeds may have as many as eight cotyledons which, when the seedling emerges, resemble the leaf (or needles) of the mature plant.

Embryos are easily seen in larger seeds such as beans or peas. In fact, aside from the outer covering, or seed coat, the embryo makes up the entire seed in the case of most dicots. The seed coat is easily removed after the seed has been soaked in water and all that remains is the embryo. The two "halves" of a bean or pea are the two cotyledons, which can be separated to reveal the embryonic axis with the plumule and radicle (Figure 1.2). In a cereal grain such as wheat, barley, or corn, representative of monocot seeds, the "fingernail" at one end of the seed is the embryo (Figure 1.3). In these seeds, the embryonic axis and the single cotyledon can be distinguished only under the microscope. In monocots, the function of the single cotyledon, also called the **scutellum**, is to facilitate the release of nutrients from the **endosperm** and their transfer to the embryonic axis. The embryos of cereal grains, especially wheat and oat, are often referred to as germ. Wheat germ is commonly sold in health food stores because it is rich in vitamins (especially vitamin E) and linoleic acid.

The largest volume of a monocot seed, again represented by the cereal grains, consists of a tissue called the endosperm. In most seeds, the endosperm consists of non-living cells filled

Relationships: A Word about Plant Diversity

About 250 years ago, Swedish professor and naturalist Carolus Linnaeus published a major work, *Species Plantarum*. At that time, the task of classifying the known organisms was relatively straightforward; organisms were either plants or animals and the distinctions between the two were obvious. Linnaeus' contribution was that he introduced a new and simplified system for describing and naming plants. But as new organisms were discovered, it was obvious that many did not fit comfortably into the two broad categories of plants and animals. Since the early part of the 20th century, a lot of study and thought has been given to the classification of biological organisms and over the years a number of different systems have been proposed. The intent has always been to place organisms into groups that reflected similar characteristics and evolutionary relationships.

One widely accepted classification system recognizes five major groups or kingdoms: Monera (bacteria), Protista (protozoans, or one-celled "animals" and photosynthetic protists, or algae), Animalia (multicellular animals), Fungi, and Plantae (plants). The five kingdoms differ fundamentally with respect to characteristics such as architecture, motility, and modes of nutrition.

Plants are further subdivided between vascular plants and non-vascular plants. The distinction between the two is that vascular plants (*L. vasculum* meaning small vessel) contain specialized conducting, or vascular, tissues for transporting water and organic solutes between various organs. Non-vascular plants, of course, do not have such specialized conducting tissues.

Non-vascular plants are grouped within a single division, Bryophyta, which includes liverworts, hornworts, and the mosses and is represented by about 16,000 species.

There are nine divisions of vascular plants, but only three divisions are represented by significant numbers of species. The division Pterophyta includes the ferns, represented by about 12,000 species. The remaining two divisions, Coniferophyta and Anthophyta, make up the majority of plants that you will likely encounter in your everyday experiences and encompass plants that are commonly referred to as seed plants.

The division Coniferophyta is the most familiar group of plants commonly referred to as gymnosperms. The conifers include the pines, spruces, firs, and redwoods. The significant feature of the conifers is that the ovules and seeds are born exposed on the cone scales.

The division Anthophyta includes all of the angiosperms or flowering plants. The significant feature of the flowering plants is, of course, that the ovules are enclosed within the flower and the seeds are enclosed within a fruit. The success of the flowering plants is reflected in the large number of species. There are approximately 235,000 species of angiosperms.

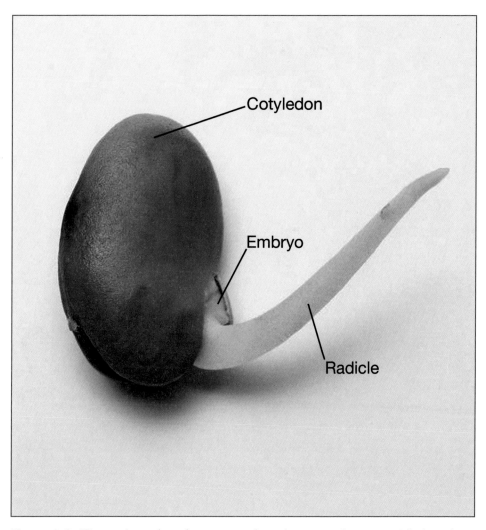

Figure 1.2 The embryonic axis emerges from between the two cotyledons in a germinating bean seed.

predominantly with starch along with smaller amounts of protein and oils. All seeds have an endosperm that is formed at the time of fertilization along with the embryo and provides nutrients to the embryo as it develops. In the monocots, the endosperm is retained in the mature seed and will continue to be a source of nutrients for the young seedling until its leaves have

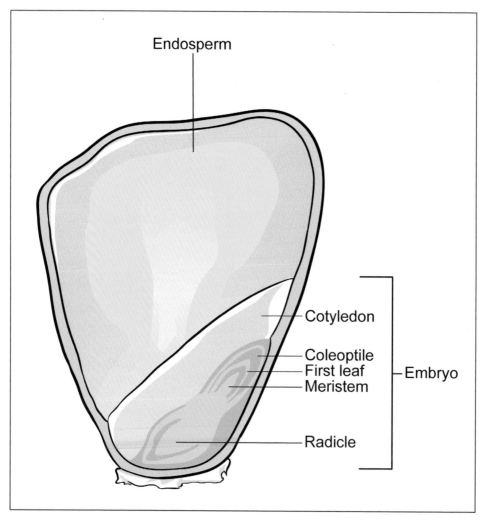

Figure 1.3 This corn seed diagram illustrates the structure of the seed. The "fingernail" at the base of the seed is the embryo, which consists of the cotyledon, coleoptile, first leaf, meristem, and radicle.

expanded and are able to carry out photosynthesis. The starchy endosperm forms the bulk of seeds such as corn and wheat. In most dicots, however, the endosperm is consumed by the embryo as it develops within the ovary and at maturity, the cotyledons are the dominant seed part. In seeds without endosperm, the cotyledons take over the role of providing nutrients for the developing seedling until it is capable of fulfilling its needs through photosynthesis. The food storage tissue in conifer seeds is technically not endosperm because it has a different origin—it is actually maternal tissue. However, its role as a nutritive tissue is the same as that of the endosperm in flowering plants.

SEEDS COME IN A RANGE OF SIZES

The seeds of some plants are very small and others are very large. The smallest seeds are produced by the orchids, one of the world's largest plant families. Some orchids have flowers the size of the head of a pin, whereas others have flowers that measure more than 20 cm (8 inches) across. Each flower produces millions of seeds that are so minute that they look like dust. The seeds are dispersed by wind and can travel hundreds of miles. Each orchid seed contains a tiny embryo but virtually no endosperm. Without endosperm to nourish the growing embryo, orchid seeds cannot germinate on their own. Instead they form a close relationship with a fungus that substitutes for the endosperm and provides the sugars and other nutrients necessary to support germination. Commercial growers avoid this problem by germinating the seeds on agar (a gelatinous medium) that incorporates sugars. At the other end of the scale are the coconuts, the seed of the coconut palm. Coconut seeds are formed within a fibrous husk that is actually a fruit. The husk is usually removed before being shipped to markets, leaving the large seed, which weighs several pounds and is encased in a stony shell. Both the milk and the meat of the coconut are endosperm. Coconut fruits are very buoyant and commonly disperse by floating to distant islands.

GERMINATION

When a seed reaches maturity, the growth of the embryo is arrested and the entire seed dries out. Under favorable conditions, however, the embryo will resume growth and emerge from the seed, a process called germination. For all seeds there are three fundamental conditions that must be met before germination can begin. First, there must be an adequate supply of water to rehydrate the desiccated seed tissues. Second, there must be a supply of oxygen to support respiratory metabolism, which provides energy and carbon for the young seedling as it develops. Third, the temperature must be within a range that allows metabolism and growth to proceed (usually 20° to 25°C, or 68° to 77°F). This range of temperatures is often referred to as "physiological temperature." Seeds that will not germinate simply because one or more of these minimum conditions have

Food for Thought

How many seeds have you eaten today? Seeds are a staple in the human diet, although we often process them to the point where we no longer recognize them as seeds when we eat them. We chop, grind, and cook them. Just take a walk through the grocery store and see how many products you can find that are made from seeds.

Beans, peas, and corn are all seeds, of course. Oatmeal is simply oat seed that has been steamed and rolled flat. Corn flakes, bread, pasta, and pie crusts, to name a few, are made from flour produced by grinding corn and cereal grains. Many seeds, such as corn, soybean, canola, cottonseed, and peanuts, are sources of oils used for cooking as well as the manufacturing of margarines and other shortenings. The oils are pressed from the embryo.

Corn and soybeans are rivals as ingredients that go into industrial food production. Soybean seeds are not a popular vegetable in North America, but soybean is a basic food in many parts of Asia. Soy protein is used to make bean curd, a staple in many Asian diets. Soybeans contain close to 45% protein and, with the exception of plants high in methionine, contain a better balance of amino acids than most plant proteins. Soybean seeds not been met are considered **quiescent**. Most seeds in the packets that you purchase to plant in your garden are simply quiescent.

Normal metabolic activities cannot be carried out without water, so the first step in germination is the absorption of water by the seed. The process by which dry materials such as seeds take up water is called **imbibition**, which occurs because water is attracted to cellulose, proteins, and other macromolecules. The molecules actually become coated with layers of water several molecules deep. The water occupies volume, of course, so when seeds imbibe water they swell. The swelling seed generates enough force to rupture the surrounding seed coat. The forces generated by imbibition can be substantial. It is believed, for

are, however, a "hidden" part of North American diets. Soybean meal, the starch and protein that remains after the seed has been pressed to extract the oil, is used in sausages, hamburgers, vegetable burgers, synthetic bacon bits, and many other food products.

Corn, however, cannot be rivaled when it comes to industrial uses. As far back as 2,400 years ago, corn had already become a staple grain throughout the Americas. In addition to being eaten as a fresh vegetable, corn is a major source of oils used in cooking, starch as a thickening agent, and corn syrup. More recently, cornstarch has become increasingly important in the manufacturing of liquid sweeteners such as fructose, which is 75% sweeter than table sugar (sucrose). High-fructose sweeteners are used in many processed foods including soft drinks and baked goods.

Aside from its food value, corn oil and starch are major feed stocks in the manufacturing of thousands of non-food industrial and consumer products including plastics, paints, and cosmetics. Corn sugars and starch are also fermented to produce ethanol as an automotive fuel additive, and refined seed oils, known as biodiesel, can be burned in diesel engines.

example, that the builders of the pyramids in Egypt quarried the rock by first driving dry wooden stakes into cracks and then pouring water on the stakes. As the wood imbibed the water, the forces generated were sufficient to split the rock.

The imbibition of water is followed by a general activation of metabolism. Exactly what triggers germination is not known, but one of the first measurable events is the onset of cellular respiration. This is closely followed by the activation of enzymes that digest the starches and other molecules stored in the endosperm, as well as activation of growth hormones that stimulate renewed cell division and cell enlargement in the embryo.

The first visible sign of germination is the emergence of the radicle, or embryonic root, from within the confines of the seed coat (see Figure 1.2). As the radicle elongates, it anchors the seed in the soil and begins the uptake of water and nutrients necessary to support the subsequent development of the young seedling.

DORMANT SEEDS HAVE SPECIAL CONDITIONS

There are many seeds that will not germinate, even though the minimum conditions of water, oxygen, and temperature have been met. These seeds are not quiescent but are considered dormant. **Dormancy** means that there are additional conditions that must be satisfied before germination can proceed. Many weed seeds, for example will not germinate unless the moist seed is exposed to light. Other seeds are immature when shed from the parent plant and require an extended period of maturation, called **after-ripening**, before they will germinate. After-ripening is often triggered by low temperature, such as it is in the seeds of apple and similar fruits. Seeds of apple, cherry, peach, walnut, and some maples will not germinate unless the moist seed is held at temperatures just above freezing for periods of two to six months. Commercial growers encourage germination of these species by placing moistened seeds in refrigerators, a process called **stratification**. The need for stratification ensures that the seed germinates the following spring, rather than germinating precociously in the fall when the seedling would not have time to become established before winter.

Some seeds have very hard seed coats that limit the uptake of water or oxygen and will not germinate until the seed coat has been disrupted, a process called **scarification**. In the laboratory or garden, scarification can be achieved by nicking the seed coat with a knife, file, or sandpaper. In nature, scarification may be achieved by the action of sand or fungi. Many seeds are scarified as they pass through the gut after being eaten by an animal. The seed not only survives the journey, but its germination is enhanced because the acid in the animal's gut has weakened the seed coat. In plant physiology laboratories, morning glory seeds are commonly soaked in concentrated sulfuric acid (a treatment called acid scarification) for up to an hour in order to improve the rate and uniformity of their germination. Seed coats of some desert species contain growth inhibitors that must be leached out by desert rains before the seed will germinate.

Seed dormancy mechanisms are of great survival value to the species. After-ripening, for example, ensures that the seeds do not germinate when freshly shed in the fall but wait until spring when seedling survival is much more likely. Scarification in an animal gut ensures widespread dispersal of the seed. The need to leach inhibitors from the seed coats of desert species ensures that the seeds germinate only during infrequent desert rains when there is sufficient water for the seeding to become established.

Pine seeds cannot germinate until the cone scales separate, which allows the seed to be released. In most species, the cones simply dry out on their own, but in species such as jack pine (*Pinus banksiana*) that have serotinous cones, the cones are impregnated with a resinous material that keeps the cones closed for many years on live trees. The scales remain closed until subjected to extreme heat, usually by a forest fire. The fire does not consume the cones, which are high on the tree, but the heat melts the resin and dries out the cones sufficient for the cone scales to open and release the seeds once the fire has passed. For this reason, jack pine is often the first tree species to repopulate burned-over areas in north central United States and Canada. These are just some examples that illustrate how germination strategies of seeds are closely linked to survival in their particular ecological niche.

SUMMARY

The life cycle of a plant begins with the seed, a quiescent structure that contains an embryonic plant (the embryo) packaged

How Long Can Seeds Survive?

In 1879, W.J. Beal, a Michigan State University scientist, buried the seeds of 20 common Michigan weeds to determine their longevity. The seeds were buried in moist, well-aerated sand and were periodically sampled to test for viability. The sampling was continued by Beal's successors and, when the study was terminated after 100 years, the seeds of three species were still viable. The record for longevity, however, is claimed by seeds of the lotus plant (*Nelumbo nucifera*) found in a peat deposit in Manchuria. Radiocarbon dating placed the age of the seeds at about 2,000 years, yet when the seed coats were scarified and the seeds moistened, all the seeds germinated.

Many other seeds are much shorter lived, remaining viable for as little as a few days or at most a year. The seeds of silver maple, for example, lose viability rapidly and must find a suitable germination medium within a few days. Seeds with large, fleshy cotyledons, such as hickories, pecans, oaks, chestnuts, and walnuts also lose viability if allowed to dry after ripening.

with nutrient tissue (the endosperm) and encased within a protective layer of maternal tissue (the seed coat). Seeds range in size from the minute, "powdery" seeds of the orchid family to seeds the size of coconuts.

Mature seeds are very dry and exhibit no signs of metabolic activity—they are in a state of suspended animation. Many seeds will germinate if the tissues are rehydrated in the presence of oxygen at physiological temperature. Germination is marked by a resumption of metabolism and growth of the embryo. The first visible sign of germination is the emergence of the embryonic root, the radicle, from within the seed coat.

Many seeds will not germinate unless special conditions have been met. Such seeds are considered dormant. Whatever the mechanism, seed dormancy ensures that seeds do not germinate precociously, that conditions are appropriate for survival of the emergent seedling, and that germination is spread over time to ensure survival of the species. Germination strategies are an important key to survival of individual species.

2 Early Seedling Development

For a tree to become tall
it must grow tough roots among the rocks.

— Friedrich Nietzsche (German classical Scholar,
Philosopher and Critic of culture, 1844–1900.)

Early Seedling Development

FROM RADICLE TO ROOT

The embryonic radicle that emerges from the germinating seed soon becomes the primary root, which continues to grow downward into the soil. The primary root is made of four principal tissues (a tissue is a complex system of different cells that work together to perform a common function). The core of the root contains the **vascular tissue**, a tissue that is highly specialized for transporting water and nutrients (Figure 2.1). Surrounding the vascular tissue is the **cortex**, a relatively undifferentiated tissue that functions primarily as a storage tissue. The cortex is in turn surrounded by the protective "skin" of the root, or the **epidermis**. Covering the very tip of the root is the **root cap**, a sheath of largely dead cells that provides mechanical protection for the actively dividing cells at the root tip. The cells at the surface of the root cap slough off as the root tip moves through the abrasive soil.

Roots serve several functions. The first is to anchor the seed—and eventually the entire plant—in the soil. The second is to absorb water and nutrients that are available only in the soil but are required by the shoot that grows above the soil. A third function, in biennial and perennial plants for example, is to store sugars, starch, or other organic nutrients through the winter. In the spring, these nutrients are mobilized and translocated to the overwintering shoot, where they provide energy and carbon for the expanding buds.

PRIMARY ROOTS GROW DOWN

Invariably, the radicle that emerges from the seed grows down into the soil; it never grows up (Figure 2.2). No matter how hard you might try, for example, a seed cannot be planted upside down. Regardless of the orientation of the seed, the primary root always turns down. But where do primary roots get this uncanny ability to distinguish down from up? Roots have an innate capacity to respond to the force of gravity, a phenomenon called

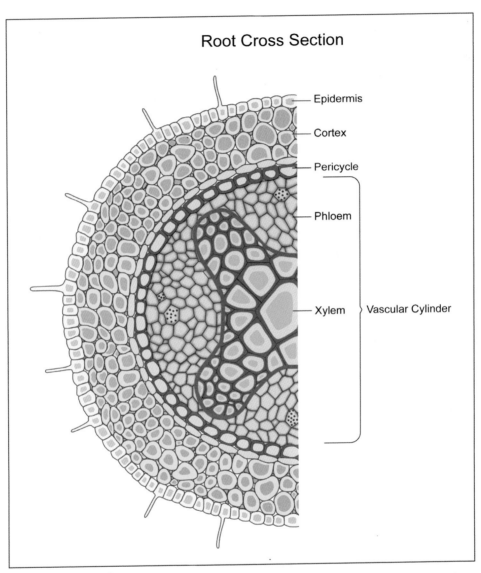

Root Cross Section

Epidermis

Cortex

Pericycle

Phloem

Xylem

Vascular Cylinder

Figure 2.1 A root typically contains a central core of vascular, or conducting, tissue surrounded by an undifferentiated cortex, and an outer skin or epidermis. The vascular cylinder contains the phloem and xylem.

gravitropism. A tropism is a response in which the direction of growth is determined by the direction of a particular stimulus. In this case, the stimulus is gravity, hence gravitropism. Roots

Figure 2.2 These corn seeds were germinated so that the roots were growing vertically. After four days, the seedlings were rotated to the horizontal position. Within three hours, the roots had again turned to resume a vertical orientation.

grow in the direction of gravity; therefore their response is called *positive* gravitropism. Gravitropism in roots is a complex response involving starch grains and a plant growth hormone called **auxin**. We will have more to say about auxin and other plant hormones in the next chapter, but for now it is sufficient to know that auxin is a hormone that controls the growth of plant cells.

Gravitropism depends on the pattern of auxin flow through the root (Figure 2.3). The hormone is produced in the epicotyl

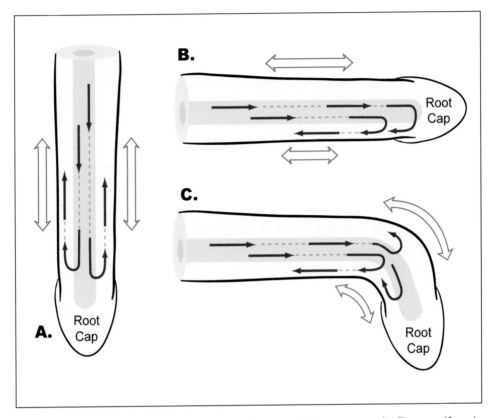

Figure 2.3 In a vertically-oriented root, the growth hormone auxin flows uniformly through the cortex, where it stimulates elongation of the root cells. When the root is oriented horizontally, the auxin flows preferentially to the lower side, where the high concentration inhibits elongation. The differential in growth between the upper and lower sides causes the root to turn down.

or the shoot and flows down into the root through the central vascular tissue. When the auxin reaches the tip of the root, it flows back up into the cortex, where it stimulates the cells to elongate. When the root is oriented vertically, the auxin flows uniformly into the cortex around the circumference of the root, all the cells elongate at the same rate, and the root continues to grow down into the soil. When the root is oriented horizontally, however, the auxin flow is redirected preferentially into the cortex on the *lower* side of the root. Now it turns out that root cells are particularly sensitive to auxin and only a very small amount is required to stimulate their elongation. In fact, too much auxin will actually inhibit root cell growth, which happens when the root is oriented horizontally. The accumulation of auxin on the lower side inhibits the growth of those cells relative to the cells on the upper side. This difference in growth between the upper and lower sides causes the root to turn down as it grows until it again assumes a vertical orientation and the normal flow of auxin is restored.

Gravity is an external signal that originates in the environment. A plant can respond to such an external signal only if it has (a) a mechanism for sensing that signal and (b) a mechanism for translating that signal into the appropriate physiological response. In the case of gravitropism, for example, plant roots must have some way of sensing gravity and then translating that information into changes in the pattern of auxin flow through the root. The gravity sensor in roots cannot be the hormone itself, because auxin is a very small molecule. The mass of auxin is much too small for it to settle through the very viscous cytoplasm in response to gravity. But root cells do contain starch grains. By cellular standards, starch grains are large and heavy. Microscopic studies have confirmed that starch grains, especially those in the root cap, do indeed settle toward the lower side of root cells when the roots are placed in a horizontal position. Other studies with starch-free mutants have shown that roots that are unable to form starch grains also do not exhibit a gravitropic response. So it seems that starch grains are part of the gravity-sensing mechanism.

According to the current model for gravitropism in roots, the response begins when starch grains, called **statoliths**, settle in response to gravity. The pressure of the starch grains on cellular membranes stimulates the release of electrically charged hydrogen ions (protons, or H^+) and calcium ions (Ca^{2+}), which accumulate in the cell walls and the spaces between the cells (the intercellular spaces) on the lower side of the root. In response to the accumulation of positively charged particles, auxin (which is a negatively charged molecule) preferentially diffuses into the lower side of the root. The difference in auxin concentration between the upper and lower sides of the root causes the required difference in growth that in turn causes the root to grow downward.

Once the primary root has established itself, branches, or secondary roots, begin to appear. Secondary roots originate as a small bud in a ring of cells, the **pericycle**, at the outer edge of the central core of vascular tissue in the primary root (see Figure 2.1). The bud originates deep inside the root, so the new vascular tissue in the branch root is able to maintain continuity with the vascular tissue in the primary root. As the secondary root elongates, it pushes through the cortex and finally breaks through the epidermis. Secondary roots are not as sensitive to gravity as are primary roots. Secondary roots may grow off at an angle or even horizontally. No one knows why secondary roots behave this way but this behavior clearly benefits the plant. The differing sensitivity of primary and secondary roots allows the roots to fill the available soil volume and thus maximize the capacity of the entire root *system* to mine the soil for water and inorganic nutrients.

SHOOTS GROW UP!
While the root system has begun to penetrate the soil, the embryonic shoot has also begun to grow. There are several patterns of early shoot development. We will start with the common bean, a plant familiar to most young students who have participated in a school science fair project. Elongation of the shoot axis in a bean embryo begins with a region that lies between the radicle and the point at which the cotyledons are attached (Figure 2.4). This region of the embryonic axis lies *below* the point at which the cotyledons are attached, so it is called the **hypocotyl**. As the

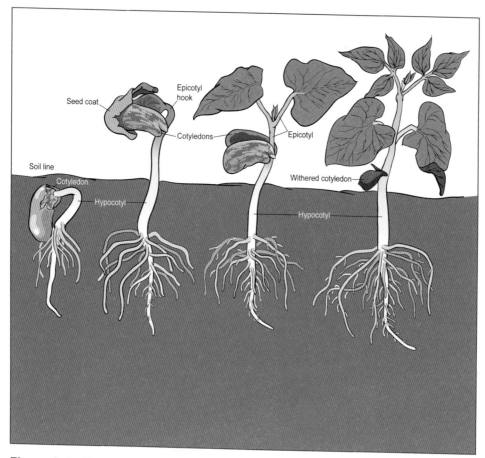

Seed coat

Epicotyl hook

Cotyledons

Epicotyl

Soil line

Cotyledon

Hypocotyl

Withered cotyledon

Hypocotyl

Figure 2.4 The stages of germination and early seedling development in the common bean begin with the elongation of the hypocotyl. The cotyledons are pulled through the soil to protect the epicotyl's leaves. Once the hypocotyl emerges from the soil, the cotyledons spread apart and reveal the epicotyl. This is an example of epigeal germination.

hypocotyl elongates, it is re-curved or bent back on itself so that the cotyledons are *pulled* rather than *pushed* through the soil. This keeps the cotyledons clasped together and protects the epicotyl's very fragile primary leaves, which lie between the cotyledons. If the cotyledons were instead to be pushed through the soil they would spread apart, thus exposing the epicotyl and primary leaves to mechanical damage. Once the hypocotyl reaches the soil surface, the hook straightens out, the cotyledons spread apart, and the epicotyl is exposed to air and sunlight. Throughout this period of growth, the bean seedling has drawn upon the food stored in the cotyledons for its nourishment. Although the cotyledons may turn green once they break through the soil surface, they contribute very little in the way of photosynthesis. The cotyledons have been drained of their nutrients and will soon wither and dry up. As the primary leaves expand, a chlorophyll precursor called **protochlorophyll** is converted to chlorophyll, the chloroplasts begin active photosynthesis, and the seedling becomes an independent, photoautotrophic organism. This pattern of early seedling development in which the

Roots and Shoots in the Microgravity of Space

One of the more intriguing questions facing plant scientists today is how plant growth, and especially gravitropism, responds to the microgravity of space. What do you expect might happen to a root and shoot in the weightless conditions of space? This topic is of more than casual interest, since astronauts may find it useful or even necessary to grow vegetables or herbs during missions.

The first seeds of wheat and corn were sent into space on Sputnik 4 in 1960. Since then, numerous experiments with seeds and young seedlings have been conducted on both manned and unmanned spaceflights. In most cases, the seedlings exhibited various abnormalities such as reduced growth and chromosomal aberrations. It was not until 1982 that a plant (*Arabidopsis thaliana*) was successfully carried through a complete life cycle—from seed to seed—in space.

Currently, several laboratories in the United States and Europe are conducting ground-based experiments in concert with the National Aeronautics and Space Administration (NASA) and other space agencies. They are developing space garden modules and other systems for future experiments on the International Space Station.

cotyledons are drawn above ground, illustrated by the bean, is described as **epigeal**.

The pea exhibits a **hypogeal** type of early seedling development in which the hypocotyl does not elongate, the cotyledons remain in the soil where they eventually decompose, and the epicotyl elongates and pulls the plumule above the soil (Figure 2.5). Note that in this case the epicotyl exhibits a pronounced hook and the embryonic leaves are pulled through the soil. Again, this serves to protect the leaves from soil abrasion.

The shoot of monocot seedlings, especially the grasses, is a bit different from dicot shoots. First of all, the single cotyledon always remains with the seed in the soil and continues to extract nutrients from the endosperm until the stored reserves are exhausted. Second, the first leaf or primary leaf of a grass seedling is enclosed within a hollow sheath called the **coleoptile**. The coleoptile is an interesting structure in its own, as we shall see in later chapters, but its primary function is to enclose and protect the fragile primary leaf, which remains rolled up inside it. The coleoptile and its enclosed leaf are pushed up through the soil by a section of the embryonic axis called the **mesocotyl** (Figure 2.6). As the coleoptile emerges from the soil, it stops growing and splits open, thus allowing the primary leaf to emerge into the light, where it unrolls and expands.

Just as the root responds to gravity by always growing down, the shoot responds to gravity by always growing up. The shoot thus exhibits *negative* gravitropism. You can test this easily by simply laying a potted plant on its side. After a few hours the tips of the shoots will start turning upwards. Unfortunately, the mechanism for shoot gravitropism is not well understood, especially in green stems. The basis for the change in orientation is similar to the root in that it is due to unequal growth. In the case of the shoot, cells on the underside grow longer than those on the upper side. Auxin is manufactured in the shoot apex and flows down the stem. The favored theory is that the unequal growth is caused by

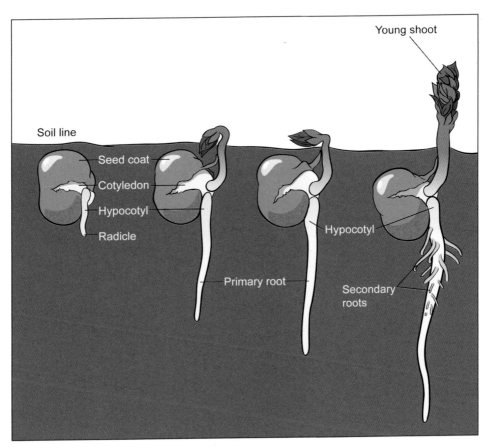

Figure 2.5 The stages in germination and early seedling development in a garden pea exemplify hypogeal germination. The hypocotyl does not elongate, the cotyledons remain in the soil, and the epicotyl pulls the plumule above the soil.

a redistribution of auxin, but attempts to detect unequal auxin distribution in horizontal shoots have not been successful.

MERISTEMS

Once the seedling has emerged from the soil, it is firmly established as a fully independent, photoautotropic organism. The seedling's root system has penetrated the soil and has begun to mine the soil for water and inorganic nutrients. The primary leaves have been elevated into the sunlight and can begin to carry

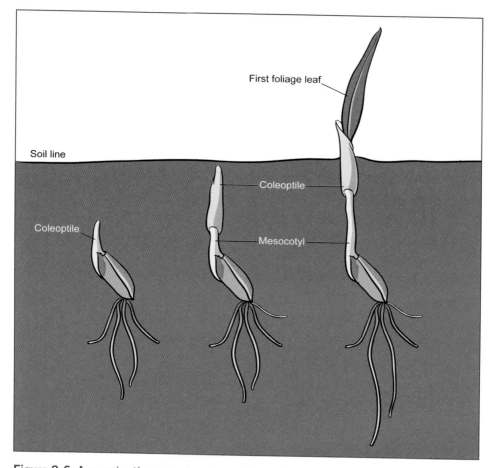

Figure 2.6 A germinating cereal grain, such as wheat or oat, protects the fragile first leaf by surrounding it with the coleoptile as it is pushed through the soil by the elongating mesocotyl.

out photosynthesis. Still, that little acorn has a long way to go to become a tall oak tree. Where and how does all that subsequent growth take place?

Unlike animals, which are characterized by a generalized growth pattern, plant growth is limited to discrete regions called meristems. Meristems are regions in the plants where the cells remain perpetually embryonic and retain the capacity for continued cell division. Two such meristems are located at the tips of roots and stems. Called **apical meristems,** these regions of active cell division are responsible for the primary growth, or the increase in the *length* of roots and stems.

The root apical meristem is a cluster of cells located at the tip of the root just behind the root cap. Within the first one to two millimeters behind the meristem is the elongation zone. In this region the elongation of the daughter cells produced by the dividing cells in the meristem push the root tip through the soil. About two to three millimeters behind the root tip begins the maturation zone. At this point the cells begin to develop the characteristic structures and functions of mature root cells. In this region as well, root hairs begin to develop. Root hairs are outgrowths of epidermal cells that extend into the capillary spaces between soil particles, where they absorb water and inorganic nutrients from the soil solution. Root hairs have such close contact with the soil particles that they are very efficient at mining the soil for water and nutrients. In fact, most of the water and inorganic nutrients extracted from the soil are taken in through the root hairs.

The shoot apical meristem is structurally more complex than the root apical meristem. This is understandable because in addition to producing new cells that extend the length of the axis of the shoot, the shoot apical meristem must also form primordia that give rise to lateral organs such as leaves, branches, and floral parts. At the same time it must perpetuate itself by maintaining a small population of undifferentiated, dividing cells. Similar to the root apical meristem, each time a cell divides in the shoot apical meristem one daughter cell is left behind to elongate and move the shoot apex forward while the other daughter cell remains within the meristem to continue dividing.

The meristem of a typical dicot shoot is a small, shiny dome that can be seen with the aid of a low-power dissecting microscope. Although the actual shape of the meristem may vary from plant to plant, the meristem of *Coleus* is fairly typical. If we slice a stem apex longitudinally and examine it under a microscope, we can see that the cells of the meristem are usually organized into two distinct regions. Cells in the outermost two to four layers, called the **tunica**, undergo only anticlinal divisions, or divisions perpendicular to the surface of the meristem. The tunica thus contributes only to surface growth. Underlying the tunica is the **corpus**, a body of cells that divide in various planes and contribute to the bulk of the shoot.

One of the ongoing mysteries of plant development is why and how leaves and branches form where they do. Part of the reason for this uncertainty is that a lot of things happen at the apex in rapid succession and it is difficult to separate various events. Leaves form as small swellings or **primordia** on the lateral flanks of the meristem. In some plants, a pair of leaf primordia will arise on opposite sides of the meristem with successive pairs arising at 90° to the last. In other plants, the leaf primordia arise in a spiral pattern. The points at which the leaf primordia form are referred to as nodes. In its early stages, the leaf primordium develops as a peg-like extension. As a leaf primordium elongates, however, marginal meristems develop on opposite sides of the primordium, leading to lateral growth that gives rise to the typical flattened blade. As each leaf primordium forms, a bud primordium is also formed in the axil where the leaf joins the stem. These axillary buds will eventually give rise to branches. While all this has been going on, cells in the regions between successive leaves, or the internodes, continue to divide and enlarge, thereby increasing the length of the stem.

The stems and roots of an oak tree grow not only in length, but also in diameter. This increase in diameter results from the activity of another meristem called the **vascular cambium** (Figure 2.7). The tissues that are derived from the root and shoot apical meristems are called **primary tissues**. The tissues laid down by the vascular cambium are called **secondary tissues**, so the vascular cambium is responsible for **secondary growth**.

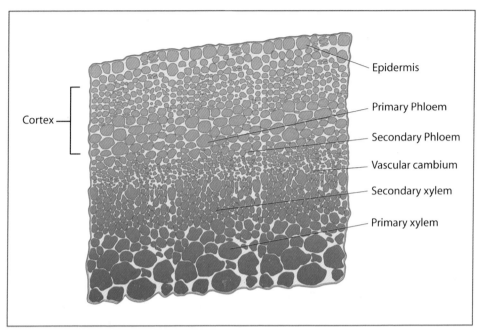

Epidermis

Primary Phloem

Secondary Phloem

Vascular cambium

Secondary xylem

Primary xylem

Cortex

Figure 2.7 The vascular cambium increases the girth of a stem by producing new xylem cells to the inside of the stem and new phloem cells to the outside of the stem.

The primary tissue contains a central core of vascular, or conducting, elements. Characteristically, the water-conducting tissue, called **xylem**, lies toward the center of the vascular core. The outer portion of the vascular core is the **phloem**, the tissue that is responsible for transporting sugars and other organic molecules. The vascular cambium develops between the xylem and phloem.

In most herbaceous (non-woody) dicots and monocots there is a limited amount of secondary growth. In woody dicots—our oak tree, for example—the vascular cambium produces new xylem toward the core of a stem (called the trunk, if it is big enough) and new phloem toward the outside of the stem every year. Xylem is a rigid and long-lasting tissue that eventually occupies the bulk of most stems or trunks. The secondary xylem that fills the bulk of a large stem or trunk constitutes what we commonly refer to as wood. Phloem, on the other hand, is a more fragile tissue and with each year's new growth the previous year's cells tend to be pushed outward and crushed. As a result, the xylem continues to transport water and minerals for several years, but a large tree seldom has more than one year's worth of functioning phloem.

The activity of the vascular cambium varies on an annual basis, producing large-diameter xylem vessels in the spring and smaller vessels in the summer. This annual cycle of activity creates the "annual rings" that provide texture to wood and allow

Wood: Nature's Original Fiber-reinforced Plastic

One of the marvels of the 20th century is the introduction of fiber-reinforced plastic composite materials in which fibrous reinforcements are embedded in a plastic matrix. Fiber-reinforced plastics, which include materials such as fiberglass and carbon fiber, are noted for their superior strength and durability. But nature invented its own fiber-reinforced plastic—the plant cell wall.

Meristematic plant cells have very thin **primary cell walls** that are built almost entirely of randomly oriented cellulose fibers. In fact, all plant cells that are actively growing and developing are surrounded only by primary walls. The wall has to be thin and malleable for these cells to enlarge and assume specific shapes. As cells enlarge, the wall does not simply stretch to accommodate the increased volume, but the existing cellulose fibers are displaced and new fibers are inserted in order to maintain a constant thickness and strength.

Once cells have attained their final size and shape, however, and begin to mature, a much heavier and permanent **secondary wall** is laid down on the *inner* surface of the primary wall. Like the primary wall, this secondary wall is also composed primarily of cellulose but the fibers are wrapped around the cell almost like a ball of string.

the cross-section of a tree trunk to be dated. As the xylem vessels mature, a substance called **lignin** is deposited in their walls. Lignin is a very complex but tough family of chemicals. In combination with the cellulose of the cell walls, lignin is what gives wood its unique characteristics.

Of course, when you look at an oak or other large tree what generally catches your eye, other than the leaves, is the **bark** or the thick outer covering of the trunk and stems. Bark is produced by yet another meristem called the **cork cambium**. The cork cambium arises just under the epidermis that originally covered the young stem or root. In an older stem, the cork cambium lies just outside

Wood, which occupies all but the outermost region of woody stems and tree trunks, consists primarily of water-conducting xylem vessels. The xylem cells are arranged in long columns, which, as they mature, lose their protoplasm to form empty, hollow, interconnected tubes.

As part of the maturation process, the cellulose fibers of xylem vessel secondary walls become impregnated with a substance called lignin. In spite of its abundance—it makes up as much as 25% of the composition of wood—the exact chemical nature of lignin is complex and not fully understood. Lignin is composed primarily of alcohol subunits that are cross-linked in a complex fashion to form very large, highly branched polymers with properties similar to many plastics. Lignin is insoluble in water and most organic solvents and is almost impossible to extract without extensive degradation. Lignin is not a desirable component of paper and its solubility properties make its extraction the most difficult and chemically intensive process in the pulp and paper industry.

Lignin also forms extensive cross links with cellulose, which is a form of carbon fiber. The result is a strong, naturally buoyant, and highly elastic fiber-reinforced plastic composite that we call wood.

the crushed, nonfunctional phloem. Cork cambium is an interesting meristem with unusual growth patterns. In most trees it may arise in a localized area, persist for a few years, and then be replaced by a new cork cambium that arises nearby. The actual pattern of activity is generally unique to each species and is responsible for the complex patterns in the outer bark that can be used to identify trees.

Strictly speaking, bark comprises everything outside the vascular cambium, *including the phloem*. For this reason bark can be easily peeled off most trees; the vascular cambium is a weak layer that enables the phloem to be easily separated from the underlying xylem. The removal of a complete ring of bark, called girdling, has dire consequences for the tree because it interrupts the continuity of the phloem and, consequently, the flow of sugars from the leaves to the roots. The roots effectively starve to death and death of the aboveground portions of the tree soon follows.

Commercial cork is harvested from the cork oak (*Quercus suber*), a native of the Mediterranean region. In this case, however, the bark is stripped not at the vascular cambium but at the cork cambium, leaving the phloem and sugar transport to the roots intact. A new cork cambium then forms just millimeters below the site of the original one and in 10 years or so, a new layer of cork is ready to be stripped. Again a new cork cambium is formed and the process repeats itself. A healthy tree may be stripped of its cork at 10-year intervals until the tree is 150 years old.

SUMMARY

A germinating seed first extends the embryonic root or radicle into the soil to anchor the seed and begin the process of absorbing water and mineral from the soil. At the same time, elongation of the embryonic axis—the hypocotyls, epicotyl, or mesocotyl—brings the shoot apex above the soil line where the first leaves expand and turn green as they accumulate chlorophyll and begin photosynthesis.

The orientation of the root and shoot during germination and subsequent growth is determined by gravitropism. The primary root is positively gravitropic and grows down, whereas the shoot is negatively gravitropic and grows upward. Gravitropism in roots begins with the settling of starch grains or statoliths in root tip cells in response to gravity. The statoliths initiate a chain of events that leads to an unequal distribution of the growth hormone auxin in the cells of the elongation zone of the root. The accumulation of auxin on the lower side of the root inhibits elongation relative to the upper side and the root turns downward. The mechanism for gravitropism in green shoots is less understood, but the shoot turns up because cells on the lower side elongate more than cells on the upper side.

Once the seedling is established, subsequent growth results from localized centers of cell division called meristems. Apical meristems at the apex of roots and shoots contribute to the increase in length of the plant axis, while lateral meristems such as the vascular cambium and cork cambium contribute to increases in diameter.

3 Hormones: Cells Talking to Cells

*The uniformity of earth's life, more astonishing than its diversity,
is accountable by the high probability that we derived, originally,
from some single cell, fertilized in a bolt of lightning as the earth cooled.*

— Lewis Thomas (American Physician
and Writer, 1913–1993)

Hormones: Cells Talking to Cells

HORMONES ARE CHEMICAL MESSENGERS

Multicellular organisms, whether plant or animal, are complex machines and the activities of individual cells and groups of cells must be coordinated and integrated so that the whole organism grows and develops according to the overall genetic plan. One way of coordinating development is with chemical messengers that pass between cells, telling cells when to turn certain activities on or off. These chemical messengers that allow cells to communicate with each other are called **hormones.**

There are five groups of plant hormones: auxins, **gibberellins, cytokinins, ethylene,** and **abscisic acid.** Each has a specific role to play in various developmental responses (Figure 3.1). These five classes of chemicals are considered hormones because they (1) are naturally occurring organic substances that (2) operate at extremely low concentrations to (3) exert a profound influence on physiological processes. It has been estimated, for example, that the growing region of pea stems may contain as little as 35 micrograms of the hormone auxin per kilogram of tissue, yet this is enough auxin to stimulate significant cell enlargement.

One of the interesting things about hormones is that they only work on certain cells, called **target cells**, and often only at certain times in the cell's history. Hormones are recognized by target cells because only target cells produce receptor proteins that bind specifically with that hormone. In much the same way that enzymes (which are also proteins) recognize specific substrate molecules, the receptor protein is a template that exactly matches the shape of the hormone molecule. In some cases the receptor is located on the surface of the cell—on the cell membrane, for example—whereas in other cases the receptor is not encountered until the hormone is taken into the cell. In either event, the formation of a hormone-receptor complex initiates a chain of biochemical events that ultimately results in the activation of a specific enzyme or gene or in some other way alters the function of the cell.

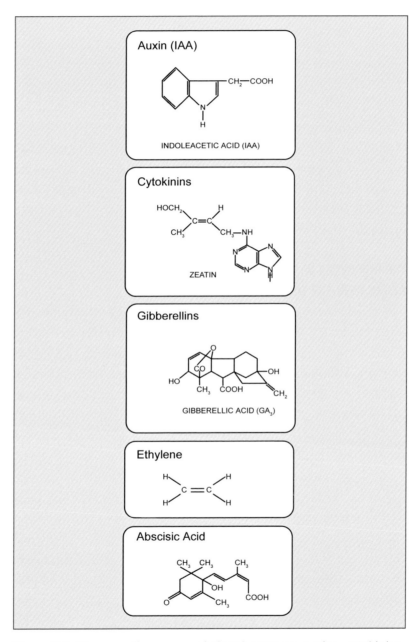

Figure 3.1 There are five groups of plant hormones: auxins, cytokinins, gibberellins, ethylene, and abscisic acid. These chemical classes are considered hormones because they occur naturally, operate at low concentrations, and exert influence on physiological processes.

The use of hormones in multicellular organisms is a particularly effective way to communicate between cells because the binding of hormones to receptor molecules is very specific. On the other hand, the biochemical mechanisms that connect the hormone-receptor complex to the final event may differ from one cell to the next. This means that the same hormone can effectively carry different messages to different cells because the hormone-receptor complex activates a different array of intracellular events in each target cell.

We will look at each class of hormones in turn: what they are, how they were discovered, and the principal role that each hormone plays in regulating plant development.

THE DISCOVERY OF PLANT HORMONES BEGAN WITH THE WORK OF CHARLES DARWIN

The classic plant hormone and the first to have been discovered is auxin, which we have already met in the previous chapter. Auxin has a storied history that goes back to the work of Charles Darwin. Although best known for his work on evolution, Darwin was also intrigued by plant behavior. In 1880, Charles Darwin and his son Francis published a book entitled *The Power of Movement in Plants*. One of the movements that captivated Darwin was the tendency of canary grass seedlings (*Phalaris canariensis*) to bend toward light coming through a window. Almost all plants exhibit this behavior, which is now called **phototropism**. Darwin observed that in young grass seedlings the coleoptile would bend toward the light. However, Darwin found that if he excluded light from the very tip of the coleoptile by covering it with a small cap made of tin foil, the coleoptile would no longer bend toward the light. When the tip of the coleoptile was exposed to unilateral light, light coming from only one side, some influence that caused the coleoptile to bend was transmitted from the tip to the lower regions of the structure.

Darwin's "transmissible influence" captured the imagination of botanists of the time and set in motion a series of experiments designed to discover its identity. In 1928, F.W. Went, then a graduate student in his father's laboratory in Holland, conducted an experiment in which he removed apical sections from oat (*Avena sativa*) coleoptiles and placed them, cut end down, on small blocks of agar. He then placed each agar block on the stump of a freshly decapitated coleoptile, but in an offset position *and in the dark*. He observed that the coleoptile bent away from the side that carried the agar block, just as though it were bending toward unilateral light as in Darwin's experiments. Clearly, Darwin's transmissible influence was a chemical substance that was able to diffuse into the agar from the excised coleoptile apex and then from the agar block into the decapitated coleoptile. This chemical then stimulated the elongation of coleoptile cells beneath the agar block, causing the coleoptile to bend. This chemical was later identified as **indole-3-acetic acid** (**IAA**), or auxin.

In the previous chapter, we saw that roots and shoots changed their direction of growth in response to gravity because of differential growth. Stems and coleoptiles bend in response to unilateral light for the same reason: cells on one side of the axis elongate more than those on the other side. This apparently occurs because unilateral light causes a redistribution of auxin as it flows down toward the base from the apex of the shoot or coleoptile where it is synthesized. Went's work revealed two very important aspects of auxin and plant growth. The first is the fundamental role of auxin in stimulating the growth of plant cells. The second is that the principal site of auxin biosynthesis is the stem apex and that auxin flows from the apex toward the base. This unidirectional flow is called **polar transport.**

AUXIN STIMULATES CELL GROWTH BY CHANGING THE PROPERTIES OF THE CELL WALL

Before looking at how auxin stimulates cell growth, we must first understand how cells grow. Cell enlargement is actually driven by the uptake of water in much the same way that a balloon or inner tube enlarges when filled with air. Cells take up water by the process of **osmosis** (see sidebar) because of the high concentration of dissolved substances in the cytoplasm and especially the large central vacuole. A cell bathed in pure water might be expected to continue to swell until the force of the expanding protoplast exceeded the strength of the surrounding cell membrane. At that point, the cell would burst and release its contents into the surrounding environment—just as a balloon or inner tube bursts when you are overzealous about inflating it. This is

Osmosis, Aquaporins, and Cell Growth

Cell membranes are selectively permeable, which means that they generally restrict the passage of dissolved substances, or solutes, while allowing the free passage of water. In fact, water moves into and out of a cell faster than almost any other molecule; the cell membrane is highly permeable to water.

The high permeability of membranes to water would not be predicted based on what is known about the properties of membranes. The basic framework of a membrane, for example, is a double layer of lipid molecules and the interior of a membrane is very hydrophobic ("water fearing"). Water is a charged molecule that is not soluble in lipids, so there is no reason to expect that a water molecule could pass freely through this lipid barrier, especially not at the rates at which water is exchanged across membranes.

Water moves freely across membranes because it does not have to interact with the lipid but flows instead through special protein-lined channels that extend from one side of the membrane to the other. These channels, called aquaporins, overcome the lipid solubility problem and permit the unrestricted flow of water through the membrane.

But why does water move in the first place? Most molecules move by diffusion. If, for example, you were to open a bottle of perfume in the corner of a room, it would diffuse from the region of high concentration (the open bottle) into the region of lower concentration (the rest of the room). Water, exactly what happens to red blood cells, for example, when they are placed in distilled water—they take up water, swell, burst, and release their contents (hemoglobin) into the solution. Plant cells would do the same thing if they were not surrounded by a very strong, rigid cell wall. The strength and rigidity of the cell wall enables them to resist deformation and to assume the special, non spherical shapes characteristic of so many plant cells. However, the presence of a rigid cell wall severely limits the capacity of the cell to grow. This is where auxin comes in. Auxin

like any other molecule, will always diffuse from a region of higher concentration to a region of lower concentration. A protoplast contains a high concentration of dissolved solutes—salts, sugars, proteins, and so forth—that take up room and displace water molecules. Cells are usually bathed in a volume of water that has a much lower concentration of dissolved substances, so the concentration of water outside the cell is always higher than the concentration of water inside the protoplast. The concentration gradient for water therefore favors its diffusion across the cell membrane into the protoplast. The diffusion of water across a selective membrane in response to a concentration gradient is called osmosis.

As water diffuses into the protoplast and the volume of the protoplast increases, another factor comes into play—pressure. The expanding protoplast exerts pressure against the cell wall, which is met by a corresponding but opposite pressure exerted by the wall itself (turgor pressure). When the force that tends to move water into the protoplast (osmotic pressure) is equal to the force exerted by the distended cell wall (turgor pressure), the *net* movement of water into the cell will stop. Equal but opposite forces simply cancel each other. At this point, water will still diffuse across the membrane in both directions, but the diffusion into the cell will be balanced by diffusion out of the cell and there will be no further change in volume.

modifies the strength and rigidity of the cell wall in order to permit water uptake and cell enlargement.

The strength of the cell wall is due largely to the high tensile strength of the long cellulose microfibrils that make up the wall, but the semi-rigidity of the wall is due to the presence of other linear carbohydrate molecules called **glycans**. The glycans form bonds with neighboring cellulose microfibrils, bridging the space between the neighboring microfibrils and tying them together into a semi-rigid network. This extensive cross-linking is what prevents the cellulose microfibrils from being displaced in response to the very high pressure generated against the cell wall by the expanding protoplast.

As the protoplast takes up water and begins to swell against the wall, the wall generates a counter-pressure called **turgor**. In the absence of a skeletal system like that found in animals, turgor is the force that prevents further water uptake and is responsible for keeping plant cells firm and the plant erect. A wilted plant, for example, is one that has lost too much water, allowing the protoplasts to shrink away from their cell walls and allowing the cells to lose their turgor.

In order to permit further water uptake and thus cell enlargement, it is necessary for auxin to modify the properties of the cell wall and reduce turgor. The process begins when auxin binds with a receptor on the outer surface of the cell. The auxin-receptor complex sets into play a chain of events that ultimately activates a proton pump located in the cell's plasma membrane. A proton pump is a protein complex that uses the energy of adenosine triphosphate (ATP) to pump hydrogen ions (H^+, or protons) out of the cell into the cell wall space. The large number of protons increases the acidity (lowers the pH) in the space around the cellulose microfibrils of the cell wall. The lower pH in turn activates a cell wall enzyme called **expansin**. Expansin molecules migrate slowly along the cellulose microfibrils and as they do they disrupt some of the bonds between the glycans and the cellulose. Each time a bond is disrupted (called a wall-loosening event) the cellulose microfibrils at that point are displaced ever so slightly, with a corresponding reduction of turgor. The cell then takes up a little bit of water, the protoplast swells, and the cell enlarges ever so slightly. The continuing process of glycan bonds being formed and broken allows the cell to slowly take up more water and increase in volume by little steps.

AUXIN HAS A ROLE IN OTHER DEVELOPMENTAL RESPONSES
Although its fundamental role is to regulate cell growth, auxin also has a role to play in several other developmental phenomena. One such phenomenon is called **apical dominance**, in which the presence of a terminal bud suppresses the growth of lateral buds (Figure 3.2). In many plants, the buds that form in the axils of the leaves either never develop or develop very slowly near the base of the plant. However, if the growing apex or terminal bud is removed, the axillary buds respond by developing as lateral shoots. On the other hand, if the apical bud is replaced with a bit of lanolin containing auxin, the lateral buds remain suppressed. The auxin manufactured in the growing apex suppresses axillary bud development as it flows down toward the base of the stem. A common horticultural practice is pinching off the terminal bud to release axillary buds from apical dominance to produce bushier plants.

Auxin also stimulates root development on cut stems, a common method of vegetative propagation. These are called **adventitious roots** because they form where roots do not normally form. Numerous commercial preparations, usually containing indole-butyric acid (IBA, a synthetic auxin) mixed with an inert ingredient such as talcum powder, are available as "rooting hormones." Auxin also influences the sex of flowers. Flowers may be **perfect**, a bisexual condition in which both male and female parts are present in the same flower, or **imperfect**, in which either stamens or pistils are present but not both. Auxin applied to

Figure 3.2 Apical dominance in broadbean (*Vicia faba*) seedlings exhibit hypogeal germination. On the left, the control seedling is growing normally. The seedling in the center has had the stem apex, as source of auxin, removed. This promoted the growth of axillary buds at the base of the stem. The seedling on the right has also had its stem apex removed, but the cut surface was covered with lanolin paste containing auxin and the axillary buds remain suppressed.

flowers in the early stages of development will promote female development; stamen development will be suppressed in favor of pistil development.

Finally, auxin has a role in fruit development. In a classic study, French physiologist J.P. Nitsch showed that fruit development was stimulated by auxin derived from seeds. Unlike most plants, strawberry "seeds" are borne on the surface of the "fruit," which allowed Nitsch to surgically remove the seeds at early stages of development. When he removed the seeds, the fruit failed to develop, but when he removed the seeds and applied auxin, normal fruit development was restored.

CYTOKININS

A second group of plant hormones, the **cytokinins**, were discovered in the 1950s as a result of efforts to artificially culture plant tissues. When small pieces of plant tissue were excised and placed on an agar medium containing auxin, sugars, inorganic nutrients, and vitamins, the cells enlarged but would not divide. Cell

Plant Hormones Have Many Practical Uses

Once it was clear that hormones controlled so many different developmental responses, there were a number of practical applications in horticulture, agriculture, and food production. Perhaps the best known example is 2,4-dichlorophenoxyacetic acid, or 2,4-D. 2,4-D is one of several synthetic chemicals that behave like auxin at low concentrations. At higher concentrations, 2,4-D is an herbicide that selectively kills broad-leaved weeds. 2,4-D is the principal herbicide in "weed-and-feed" fertilizers and similar lawn care products. Naphthaleneacetic acid and indolebutyric acid are two synthetic auxins that are used in commercial rooting powders to stimulate root formation on cuttings during vegetative propagation. Auxin sprays are also used to control fruit set and preharvest fruit drop in apple and pear orchards.

Gibberellins are used to stimulate elongation of grape stems. This opens up the cluster and allows larger berries to form. Virtually all of the Thompson seedless green table grapes produced in California are sprayed with gibberellins. Chemicals known as anti-gibberellins, or dwarfing agents, interfere with the biosynthesis of gibberellins in the plant. Anti-gibberellins are commonly used to reduce stem elongation and produce shorter, more compact plants in horticultural crops such as chrysanthemums and poinsettias.

Ethylene is used to ripen bananas, honeydew melons, and tomatoes. The fruit is picked before it ripens so it will withstand shipping long distances. At the wholesaler, the fruit is placed in an airtight chamber and gassed briefly with ethylene. The ripening process then begins within a day or so, in time to be placed on the grocery shelves.

division could be stimulated if the cultures were supplemented with extracts from a variety of sources including yeast, the milky endosperm of coconut, young corn seeds, and developing plum fruitlets. Naturally, scientists began searching for the "cell division factor" contained in these extracts.

As an interesting example of serendipity in science, the first active preparation was actually isolated from a sample of DNA. Early evidence indicated that the active substance in yeast extract was a purine similar to adenine, one of the building blocks of DNA, so the scientists sampled a small bottle of herring sperm DNA that had been sitting on the laboratory shelf. The sample had high cell division activity in the tissue culture assay. The next step was to purchase some new DNA and attempt to isolate larger quantities of the factor. Much to their consternation, extracts of the new DNA proved to be totally inactive! They soon discovered that the old DNA had aged while sitting unprotected on the shelf and they could generate high activity from new DNA by artificially aging it in the autoclave. Had they stored the bottle of DNA in the refrigerator 50 years ago as we do now, the story of cytokinins would have taken a very different turn.

The factor stimulated cell division, or cytokinesis, so it was named **kinetin** and the class of hormones was called cytokinins. Kinetin was, of course, manufactured from the DNA by the aging process and so is an artifact of the isolation method. However, naturally-occurring cytokinins with chemical structures similar to kinetin have since been isolated from a wide variety of plant tissues.

CYTOKININS SIGNAL THE CELL WHEN TO DIVIDE

The term cell division invariably conjures up visions of mitosis, in which the genetic material is doubled and the sister chromosomes are separated to form two identical daughter nuclei. Mitosis is followed by cytokinesis, in which the cytoplasm divides to form two identical cells. Between divisions, however, each daughter cell must increase the amount of cytoplasm as it enlarges, replicate its DNA, and prepare for the next round of mitosis. This entire sequence of events from one division to the next is known as the **cell cycle**.

The cell cycle can be described in four distinct phases with reference to the events occurring in the nucleus: the *mitotic* phase (M = mitosis), the DNA *synthesis* phase (S = synthesis) and two intervening phases or *gaps* of apparent inactivity (G1 and G2) (Figure 3.3). During the S phase, the DNA is replicated, leading to two identical copies of the chromosomes, but the chromosomes are uncoiled and not visible in the light microscope. During the G2 phase, the newly replicated chromosomes begin to coil or condense and the cell assembles the machinery necessary to move the chromosomes apart during mitosis. During the G1 phase, cells grow and function while not actually dividing. The G1 phase thus accounts for the largest portion of the cell's life span. In the absence of cytokinin, freshly established tobacco cell cultures are arrested in either the G1 or G2 phase, so the question of what controls cell division then becomes one of how cytokinin tells the cell it is time for the cell cycle to continue. In other words, how does cytokinin stimulate the transition from G1 to S or G2 to M? In the case of tobacco cell cultures, the onset of cell division can be detected within 12 to 24 hours following the addition of cytokinin. The answer to the question of what controls cell division in plant cells appears to be cytokinin.

The transitions are directly controlled by the activity of an enzyme with the somewhat imposing name of **cyclin-dependent kinase**, or **CDK**. During G1, CDK is inactive because a small activating subunit called **cyclin** is missing. One role of cytokinin is to promote the accumulation of the necessary cyclin, which then allows the G1 to S transition to proceed. Cytokinins are also involved in the G2 to M transition, but in this case cytokinin activates CDK by promoting the removal of an inhibitory group.

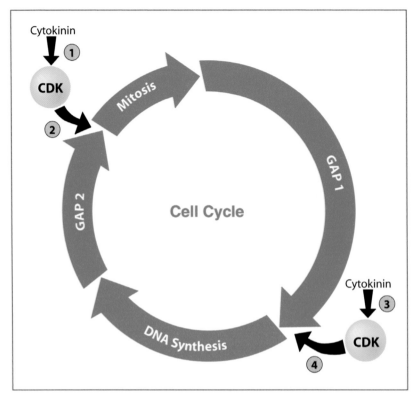

Figure 3.3 The cell cycle has four distinct phases: mitosis, DNA synthesis, and gaps of inactivity (G1 and G2). Cytokinins tell the cell when to divide by controlling DNA synthesis and the onset of mitosis.

In either case, it appears that cytokinin has a fairly direct role in regulating the progression through the cell cycle.

GIBBERELLINS REGULATE STEM ELONGATION, SEED GERMINATION, AND FLORAL DEVELOPMENT

In the early 20th century, Japanese rice farmers became increasingly concerned about a disease that reduced the yield of their rice crops. Plants infected with the *bakanae* ("foolish seedling") disease were characterized by very long, weak stems. By 1938 it was learned that the disease was caused by a fungal infection that stimulated the release of a growth stimulant. The substance was given the name gibberellin after the name of the fungus, *Gibberella fuijikuroi.* In an interesting interplay between science and world politics, gibberellin did not come to the attention of Western scientists until after the end of the 1939–1945 war when groups in both the United States and Great Britain isolated and chemically characterized the gibberellin from fungal extracts. Since then, gibberellins have been shown to be ubiquitous in higher plants.

It is probably not surprising that a principal effect of gibberellins is to stimulate stem elongation, since excessively elongated stems in rice plants was the basis for the discovery of this plant hormone. Gibberellins stimulate the elongation of internodes, which is that portion of the stem between where the leaves are attached (the nodes). The effect of gibberellins can be fairly dramatic. Indeed, a genetic deficiency in gibberellin production is the most common cause of dwarfism in plants. Many cultivars of peas, for example, contain the *Le* gene (the same gene studied by Gregor Mendel in his pioneering genetic experiments) which, in the homozygous recessive *le/le*, partially blocks the biosynthesis of gibberellins. These cultivars, such as Progress #9 or Little Marvel, are dwarf vines growing only 45 to 50 cm (18 to 20 inches) high. Non-dwarf cultivars or tall peas (heterozygous for the *Le* allele), such as Alaska or Tall Telephone, will grow as high as 75 to 150 cm (30 to 60 inches). Dwarf and tall cultivars will have approximately the same number of node (or leaves)—the dwarf cultivars simply have much shorter internodes. On the other hand, spraying the dwarf cultivars with a dilute solution of gibberellin will cause their internodes to elongate and they will be indistinguishable from genetically tall peas (Figure 3.4).

Another dramatic effect of gibberellins is control of stem elongation in rosette plants (Figure 3.5). A rosette growth habit is essentially an extreme case of dwarfism in which failure of internode elongation makes it appear that the leaves all arise from the same point. Spinach, cabbage, and head lettuce are common

Figure 3.4 The shortened internodes of the dwarf pea on the left indicate a gibberellin deficiency. The plant on the right is also a dwarf of the same age, but it shows enhanced internode elongation after it was sprayed with a gibberellin solution.

examples of rosette plants. Plants such as spinach and cabbage remain in the rosette stage unless subjected to an appropriate day length (Chapter 5) or low temperature treatment (Chapter 6). They then undergo extensive internode elongation (a phenomenon known as **bolting**), sending up a long shoot that is normally followed by the production of flowers. Alternatively, rosette plants can be induced to bolt by spraying them with a diluted solution of gibberellin. Further evidence for the role of gibberellins in bolting comes from studies showing that internode elongation in spinach

Figure 3.5 Gibberellin stimulates stem elongation in rosette plants. *Brassica napus* normally grows as a rosette habit, with no obvious stem (left). The three plants on the right were treated with 0.5, 1.0, and 10.0 nanograms (1 ng = 10^{-9} gram) of gibberellin.

following long days is correlated with the conversion of gibberellin from an inactive form to an active form.

Although both auxins and gibberellins influence stem elongation, they do so in different ways and appear to operate independently. For example, gibberellins are not involved in gravitropic or phototropic responses and auxins will not cause bolting in rosette plants.

ABSCISIC ACID
The hormone abscisic acid was originally discovered and chemically characterized through studies of inhibitors in buds and

leaves that were involved in the onset of dormancy and leaf drop (**abscission**) in woody plants. Abscisic acid has little or nothing to do with either of these phenomena but does have a prominent role in signaling water stress and regulating seed germination.

One of the more serious problems most terrestrial plants face is water stress. Leaves are covered with a waxy layer, or **cuticle**, that prevents the evaporation of water from the leaf surfaces. Unfortunately, the cuticle also prevents the exchange of carbon dioxide and oxygen that is necessary for photosynthesis. To overcome this dilemma, leaves have developed pores, called **stomata**, that can open during daylight hours so the leaf can take up carbon dioxide, but will close when necessary to prevent excessive loss of water vapor, or transpiration, from the inside of the leaf. The bulk of a plant's water supply is taken from the soil, so it would clearly be beneficial if the leaves could be notified by the roots of a potential water supply problem. In fact, the message of impending water shortage is conveyed from the roots to the leaves in the form of abscisic acid. Abscisic acid is very effective in inducing stomatal closure and when the soil begins to dry out, large amounts of abscisic acid are rapidly transported from the roots to the leaves; the stomata close, and wilting of the leaves is forestalled, at least for the immediate future.

ETHYLENE

A fourth plant hormone, ethylene, is a simple gaseous hydrocarbon that inhibits growth and stimulates ripening of fruit. Indeed, ethylene and its effects were discovered because of problems with shipping bananas. Remember the old mantra about the one rotten apple in the barrel? It had been known for a long time that overripe and rotting fruit could accelerate the ripening of other fruit stored nearby. Around the turn of the 20th century it was common for shiploads of bananas shipped from Cuba to New York to arrive overripe and unmarketable. In the 1930s it was discovered that overripe fruits, such as apples, release large quantities of ethylene gas, which in turn accelerates ripening in other, less mature fruit. In addition to its role in fruit ripening, ethylene is now known to inhibit many plant responses. It is also known that auxin can stimulate ethylene synthesis in plant cells. It is widely agreed, for example, that the inhibitory effect of auxin on the growth of root cells is actually due to ethylene that is released in response to the high auxin concentration.

SUMMARY

Hormones are molecular messengers that coordinate the development of multicellular organisms by carrying messages between cells. There are five recognized groups of plant hormones: auxins, gibberellins, cytokinins, ethylene, and abscisic acid. All of the hormones interact with each other in subtle ways to control the overall pattern of development, yet each hormone has certain prominent functions.

Auxin was the first plant hormone to be discovered. Auxins are produced in actively growing tissues, especially the shoot apices and developing fruits. Their principal activity is to stimulate cellular enlargement, which is reflected in normal elongation of the plant axis as well as in responses to environmental stimuli such as gravity (gravitropism) and uneven lighting (phototropism). Auxins also have a role in apical dominance, seed germination, and flower and fruit development.

Gibberellins stimulate the growth of stems, particularly in rosette plants. Low levels of gibberellins are responsible for dwarfism in plants and, like auxins, have a role in seed germination and flower and fruit development.

The principal role of cytokinins is to regulate cell division, whereas ethylene figures prominently in the ripening of fruits. Abscisic acid serves as the primary signal for telling leaves and shoots of impending water stress.

4 Light and Plant Development

I knew, of course, that trees and plants had roots, stems, bark, branches, and foliage that reached up toward the light. But I was coming to realize that the real magician was light itself.

— Edward Steichen

Light and Plant Development

LIGHT AND SEED GERMINATION

The instructions on the packet of lettuce seeds are clear: cover the seed with no more than 3 mm (1/8 inch) of soil. But what would happen if the seeds were planted too deeply? In all likelihood, many seeds would not germinate. This implies that a lettuce seed is able to sense its position in the soil and use that information to "determine" whether or not germination is appropriate. Now we know seeds do not have a nervous system or conscious thought, so how can a seed sense its position in the soil and "know" whether or not to germinate? The answer lies in the fact that the lettuce seed requires a light treatment before it will germinate and light does not penetrate very far into most soils—a few millimeters at best. If the seed is planted too deeply, it will not be able to detect the light that is required to stimulate germination. Lettuce seed is not alone; the same is true of many other seeds as well. Natural soils, for example, may contain many thousands of weed seeds that fail to germinate because they are buried too deeply and are unable to detect the light. It has been estimated that a hectare (about two acres) of farmland contains a **seed bank** with more than two million weed seeds that will not germinate until the soil is disturbed and the seeds are brought closer to the surface where they are exposed to light.

There is good reason for this behavior. Seeds that require light for germination are usually very small (a single one ounce or 28-gram packet of lettuce seeds may contain 20,000 seeds) and, consequently, have limited nutrient reserves. When the seed germinates, the seedling has only the store of nutrients in the seed to draw upon until it breaks through the soil and can begin photosynthesis. The light requirement is a way of telling a seed whether it is in the right position relative to the soil surface and that reserves will be sufficient to ensure the seedling is able to reach the surface. For weed seeds, there is an additional advantage; the large bank of seeds in the soil ensures survival of the species by spreading germination through successive disturbances over several years.

The control of seed germination is just one example of the many ways plants use light to regulate their development. Collectively, these responses are called **photomorphogenesis** (from *photo*, meaning light; *morphology*, meaning form; and *genesis*, meaning to give rise to). However, before we delve further into photomorphogenesis, it would help to review some fundamental principles of light.

LIGHT AS A SOURCE OF INFORMATION

The 18th century English poet, essayist, and lexicographer Samuel Johnson once said, "We all know what light is; but it is not easy to tell what it is." Light is a form of energy that has some interesting and perplexing properties. The problem arises from the observation that light consists of discrete bundles of energy that have both wave-like and particle-like properties. When light is transmitted through space it is described by regular and repetitive changes in its electrical and magnetic properties; it behaves like a wave. On the other hand, when light is emitted—as from the sun or a light bulb—or absorbed by a pigment, it behaves like a stream of particles called **quanta** or **photons**.

The peak-to-peak distance on successive waves is called the wavelength, which is normally measured in nanometers (nm = 10^{-9} m). The dual nature of light has two important and related consequences for organisms. First, different wavelengths of light are recognized by the eye and brain as different colors (Figure 4.1). Second, the energy carried by a photon is *inversely* proportional to its wavelength. In other words, a photon of long wavelength red light carries less energy than a photon of shorter wavelength blue light. In a process such as photosynthesis, the **quantum** nature of light is most important. The photosynthetic pigment chlorophyll consumes photons of energy that are eventually stored in sugar products. Up to a point, the more energy that is absorbed in photosynthesis, the more products can

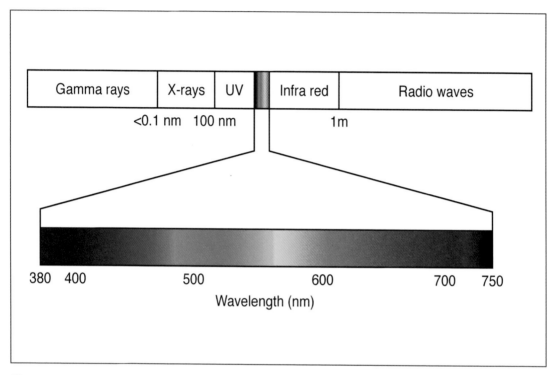

Figure 4.1 Visible light is that small portion of the electromagnetic spectrum that causes the sensation of color in the human brain.

be formed. In photomorphogenesis, the wave nature of light is more important. It is not the energy of light that drives photomorphogenesis so much as the information that is conveyed by different wavelengths of light.

Here is one example of the kind of information that may be conveyed by light. In full sunlight—such as in the middle of a field—the ratio of red light (R, nominal wavelength = 660 nm) to far red light (FR, nominal wavelength = 730 nm) is about 1.05 to 1.25. Under a canopy of trees—such as on the floor of an oak forest—the R/FR ratio drops to something around 0.12 to 0.17. Can you think of why the proportion of red light drops so dramatically in the shade? The reason is that the chlorophyll in the leaves of the canopy filter out the red light for use in photosynthesis, but chlorophyll is virtually transparent to far red light. Consequently, the canopy has changed the balance of wavelengths or **spectral composition** of the light reaching the forest floor by enriching it with far red light. A plant that has a mechanism to detect this change in red/far red ratio could use this information to determine whether it was in full sun or in the shade of a canopy and adjust its physiology and development accordingly.

In addition to canopy shade, a variety of atmospheric factors and the time of day can influence the spectral composition of light. Sunlight thus satisfies two very important needs of plants: (1) energy to drive photosynthesis and (2) providing critical information about the environment that is used by plants to regulate movement, trigger developmental events, and measure the passage of time.

Did You Know?

Visible light is only a small portion of a much larger set of electromagnetic waves called the electromagnetic spectrum. The entire spectrum ranges from the very long radio waves, with wavelengths measured in meters or tens of meters, and microwaves (0.01–1.0 m) to the very short x-rays (10^{-8} m–10^{-12} m) and gamma rays (10^{-10} m–10^{-16} m).

Visible light is that portion of the electromagnetic spectrum that stimulates the visual pigments in the human eye and is interpreted by the brain as color. Light ranges in wavelength from the short-wavelength violet end of the spectrum at 3.8×10^{-7} m (or 380 nm) to the long-wavelength red end at 7.2×10^{-7} m (or 720 nm). The wavelengths of ultraviolet light are, as the name implies, just shorter than the violet end of the visible spectrum. Photons of ultraviolet light have higher energies than visible light—high enough to cause sunburn and skin cancer. Just beyond the red end of the spectrum lies the infrared radiation, which we commonly refer to as heat.

PHYTOCHROME: A LIGHT-ACTIVATED SWITCH

In the early 1950s, Harry Borthwick and a group of coworkers at a United States Department of Agriculture laboratory decided to explore the role of light in lettuce seed germination. They kept some seeds in the dark as controls and briefly exposed others to various wavelengths (or colors) of light before returning them to darkness. The results showed that germination was stimulated primarily by a flash of red light, but they also found that a flash of far red light actually inhibited germination (Table 4.1). This observation prompted them to try a "what if" experiment: what would happen if the seeds were exposed to alternating flashes of red light and far red light? The results were quite surprising. No matter how many repeated flashes were given, if the sequence ended with a flash of red light, germination was high. If the final flash was far red light, the majority of the seeds did not germinate. It was as though germination was governed by a light-activated switch; red light switched germination on and far red light switched it off. The response was **photoreversible**!

This was a novel observation because such complete photo-reversibility was totally without precedent in biology. However, Borthwick and his coworkers went on to show that several other light-dependent plant responses exhibited similar behavior. To account for this phenomenon, they proposed that plants contained a novel pigment they called **phytochrome** (*phyto*, plant; *chrome*, pigment). They further proposed that the pigment could exist in two forms; a red-light-absorbing form called Pr and a far red-absorbing form called Pfr (Figure 4.2). The two forms are interconvertible, which means that when Pr absorbs red light it is converted to the Pfr form and when the Pfr form absorbs far red light it is converted back to the Pr form. The pigment is synthesized as Pr, which is the form that accumulates in seeds. Light causes a conversion of some of the Pr to Pfr, which induces a biological response—in this case seed germination. This proposed pigment system was so unusual that some reputable

Table 4.1 The effect of alternate red and far red light treatments on the germination of lettuce seeds.

LIGHT TREATMENTS	GERMINATION (%)
Dark Control	20%
R	88%
R, Fr	22%
R, Fr, R	84%
R, Fr, R, Fr	18%

scientists of the day considered it a "pigment of the imagination." However, a few years later Borthwick and his coworkers presented irrefutable physical evidence that such a pigment did indeed exist and it is now recognized that phytochrome has a role to play in virtually every stage of plant development.

SOME OTHER PHYTOCHROME RESPONSES

A common primary school science experiment involves germinating bean seeds in the dark (bean seeds are very large and do not require light for germination). The subsequent seedling is characterized by elongated and spindly hypocotyls with a pronounced hook at the top (Figure 4.3). The unexpanded leaves remain folded together as they were in the embryo. The hypocotyls are white and the small folded leaves are yellow. Such a seedling is said to be **etiolated** and is characteristic of seedlings that have not yet emerged from the soil.

When a bean seedling emerges from the soil into the light under normal growing conditions, the etiolated condition quickly gives way to the normal growth pattern: hypocotyl elongation slows, the hook straightens out, and the leaves expand and turn green. The same thing will happen in a dark-grown seedling

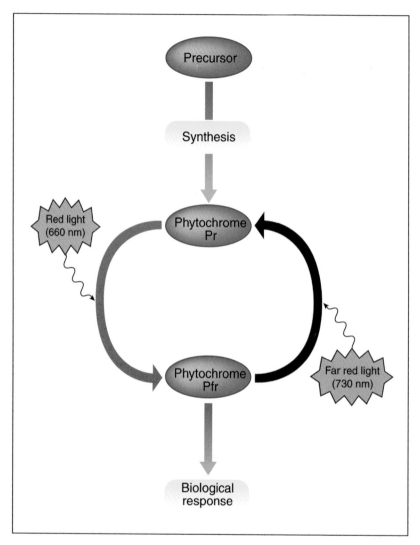

Figure 4.2 Phytochrome exists in two forms: Pr and Pfr. When Pr absorbs red light, it is converted to Pfr. When Pfr absorbs far-red light, it is converted back to Pr. In normal daylight, which contains both red and far-red light, a dynamic equilibrium is established and the plant contains a mixture of the two forms.

that is given as little as five minutes of red light daily for three days. If each red light treatment is followed by five minutes of far red light, none of these changes will occur and the seedling

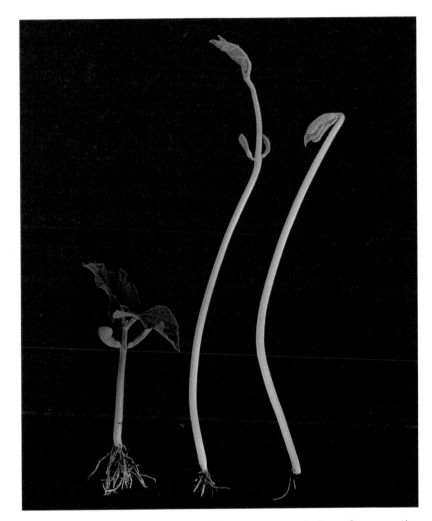

Figure 4.3 Phytochrome regulates seedling morphology. Compare the middle seedling with the dark-grown seedling on the right and the light-grown seedling on the left. The middle seedling was also grown in the dark but was exposed to five minutes of weak red light on day six. Note that a single brief exposure to red light causes the plumular hook to straighten, stimulates epicotyl elongation, initiates leaf expansion, and stimulates chlorophyll formation in the leaves. All seedlings are seven days old.

remains etiolated. Phytochrome serves as the seedling's eyes, telling it when it has emerged from the soil into the light and that it should expand its leaves to prepare for photosynthesis.

In addition to **de-etiolation**, phytochrome is also involved in the formation of the red anthocyanin pigments in apples and cabbages, the activation of numerous genes and enzymes, photoperiodic floral induction (Chapter 5), and a variety of other plant responses. Of course, normal daylight contains a mixture of red and far red light, which means that a light-grown plant will contain a mixture of Pr and Pfr and the magnitude of a particular plant response will depend on whether the pigment is poised more toward one form or the other. In other words, it is the balance between Pr and Pfr that determines how the plant responds. That is how the shade-grown plant mentioned earlier

Plants Are Exposed to an Ever-changing Light Environment

The only thing constant about the natural light environment is that it is never constant. The amount of light changes from sunrise to sunset and every time a cloud passes over.

But there are some changes in the light environment that are highly predictable on both a daily and seasonal basis. These predictable changes provide critical information about the environment—information that plants can use to their advantage. The two most important changes in visible light on a daily basis are in the quantity of energy (**fluence rate**) and the color composition (**spectral energy distribution**). Fluence rate is a measure of the number of photons (expressed as micromoles) that fall on a square meter every second. Spectral distribution refers to the wavelength composition of the light or color balance.

Typically the fluence rate increases gradually from sunrise until it reaches a maximum at midday under a full sun before again declining. At twilight, just before the sun sets, the fluence rate will have declined by 200-fold. At the same time, the spectral distribution also changes. Normal daylight is composed of both direct sunlight and diffuse, or not only "knows" it is growing under the canopy, but how thick the canopy is as well. In full sunlight, there are approximately equal amounts of Pr and Pfr while shade-light is predominantly far red and the Pr form of the pigment will dominate. Shade-grown plants consequently respond with increased stem growth, while their siblings, which grow in unfiltered daylight, tend to have shorter internodes and are more compact.

Stem length is not the only characteristic that is controlled by phytochrome. The leaves of a shade-grown plant are thinner, generally with a larger surface area, fewer cell layers, and less chlorophyll. Sun-grown leaves are smaller and thicker, with a

scattered, skylight. Light scattering occurs because moisture droplets, dust, and other impurities in the atmosphere deflect rays of light. The scattering effect is greater at shorter wavelengths, which means that diffuse skylight is enriched with blue wavelengths—hence blue skies! At sunrise and sunset, the sun's rays enter the earth's atmosphere at a much lower angle and the path traveled by the sunlight to an observer may be up to 50 times longer than it is when the sun is directly overhead. A combination of refraction (bending) when the rays enter the atmosphere and scattering—most of the blue light is scattered out of the line of sight—leaves predominantly the longer orange and red wavelengths to reach the viewer. This is why the sun is always bright orange at sunrise and sunset!

These daily changes in fluence rate and spectral energy distribution occur with great regularity and convey rather precise information about the momentary status of the environment. It should not be surprising that plants have evolved sophisticated mechanisms such as phytochrome for interpreting this information as a matter of survival.

larger number of cell layers and more chlorophyll. This enables them to efficiently utilize the larger quantity of light intercepted by leaves growing in full sun. All of these developmental responses are attributable to phytochrome.

WHAT IS PHYTOCHROME AND HOW DOES IT WORK?

Pigments are simply molecules that absorb light and phytochrome is only one of many different pigments found in plants. There are the chlorophylls that absorb light for photosynthesis and are responsible for the green color of most leaves. There are the red, orange, and yellow carotenoids that give color to tomato fruit, carrot roots, and corn kernels. There are also the anthocyanin pigments whose blues, reds, and purples color floral petals, apple skins, and the multicolored leaves of foliage plants in the house and garden.

Unlike chlorophyll, carotenoids, and anthocyanins, phytochrome is a protein or, more specifically, a **chromoprotein**. A chromoprotein is a protein with a **chromophore**, an attached group that absorbs light. Another familiar chromoprotein is the oxygen carrier in the blood, hemoglobin. Hemoglobin is red in color. If you could see phytochrome, it would be a blue color. But you cannot see phytochrome in a plant, even in an etiolated plant, because there simply is not enough. Phytochrome is present in very low concentrations, which is in keeping with its role as a regulator. The plant does not need a lot of something if it is used principally as a switch to turn other things on and off.

How does phytochrome influence development? There appear to be two possible mechanisms. The first possible mechanism involves the activation of enzymes. Enzymes are commonly present in cells in an inactive state and require activation before they can do their job. The most common way to activate enzymes is by adding a phosphate group, a process called **phosphorylation** (Figure 4.4). Scientists have recently found that a portion of the phytochrome molecule, when in the Pfr form, acts like an enzyme

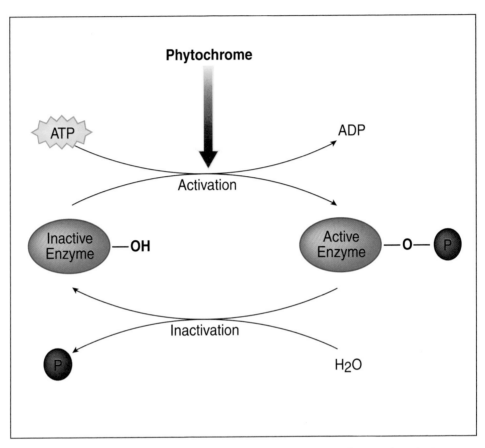

Figure 4.4 Phytochrome activates certain enzymes by adding a phosphate group from ATP. The activated enzyme then initiates a cascade of biochemical events (a signal cascade) that leads to a physiological response.

that causes phosphorylation of other proteins. Just as hormones initiate a signal cascade by binding with a receptor molecule, phytochrome could initiate a signal cascade by activating certain enzymes. Different responses would result depending on the particular enzyme that was activated by phytochrome in a particular cell at a particular time.

The second possible mechanism for phytochrome action involves the activation of genes. Whenever an overt developmental change takes place in any organism, the prevailing expectation is that changes in gene expression are involved. The participation of phytochrome in major developmental events such as seed germination, de-etiolation, and flowering naturally suggests that the pigment might regulate gene expression. Indeed, a number of proteins have been identified whose genes are expressed differently in light-grown and dark-grown plants. Experiments have now shown that inactive phytochrome (Pr) is located predominantly in the cytoplasm, but when Pr is converted to the active form (Pfr) the Pfr migrates into the cell's nucleus (Figure 4.5). There the Pfr binds with a piece of DNA called a promoter that is linked to a specific gene. The bound Pfr activates the promoter, which then turns on the target gene. If the Pfr should be irradiated with far red light, the Pfr is immediately converted to Pr, which rapidly dissociates from the DNA and cancels any further activation—a pretty neat way to turn genes on or off with a flash of light!

PHOTOTROPISM IS A RESPONSE TO BLUE LIGHT

In the previous chapter, we learned that plants respond to light coming from one side, or unilateral light, by growing toward the light. This response was called phototropism. In real life, of course, plants are seldom exposed to light from only one side; that is usually an artificial setup in the laboratory. On the other hand, plants are commonly exposed to more light from one side than the other. A house plant near a window, for example, will receive more light through the window than from the room inside. Phototropism requires only that there be a gradient of light across the shoot—that is, the light is stronger on one side than the other.

Phototropism is also a response to blue light, which means that coleoptiles and shoot apices must contain a pigment that absorbs blue light. Although phototropism has been studied intensively for the better part of a century, the responsible pigment came to light only recently. The pigment is called **phototropin** and, like phytochrome, is present in very small

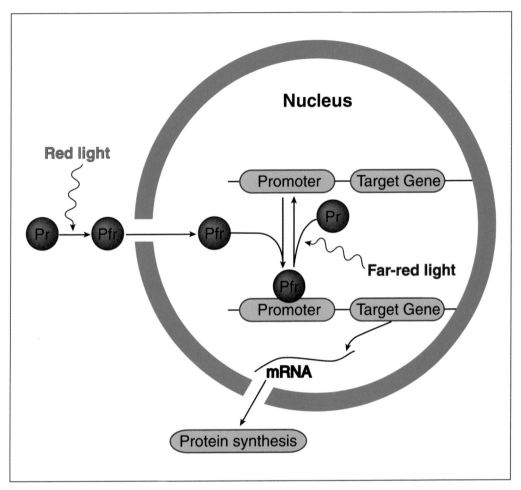

Figure 4.5 Following an exposure to red light, the Pfr form of phytochrome migrates from the cytoplasm into the nucleus, where it turns on a target gene by binding with the promoter of the gene. A far-red light treatment will convert Pfr to Pr, which dissociates from the promoter and turns off the gene.

amounts. This is one of the reasons that phototropism was so difficult to discover. Also like phytochrome, phototropin is a chromoprotein with a chromophore consisting of two **riboflavin** molecules. Unfortunately, scientists do not yet know how phototropin translates a gradient in light intensity across a plant organ into a differential growth response.

SUMMARY

Light is both a source of energy for processes such as photosynthesis and a source of information that tells a plant a great deal about its environment. The use of this information to direct plant development is called photomorphogenesis.

The pigment primarily responsible for photomorphogenesis in plants is called phytochrome. Phytochrome is a chromoprotein, which is a protein with an attached light-absorbing chromophore. The unique characteristic of phytochrome is that it exists in two forms, Pr and Pfr, which are interconvertible by light. Pr absorbs

Finding an Elusive Pigment

How does one identify a pigment that perceives light for a phenomenon like phototropism? The traditional approach to linking pigments with responses involves a basic tenet of photobiology, namely that only light that is absorbed can be effective in generating a response. By this method, the responding organ—a coleoptile, for example—is presented with different wavelengths or colors of light and the degree of response is measured. This is called an action spectrum. The action spectrum for the response is then compared with the absorption spectra—a similar measure of the amount of light that is absorbed by a pigment at different wavelengths— of possible candidate pigments. If the two match, you have found the pigment in question. This approach works well for photosynthesis, in which the action spectrum is a good match with chlorophyll, and it was instrumental in the discovery of the previously unknown phytochrome. Unfortunately, the action spectrum did not work very well in the case of phototropism. The action spectrum for phototropism (and several other blue-light responses) shows a strong response in the blue and ultraviolet regions of the spectrum, which does not match the absorption spectrum of any known pigment.

The discovery of phototropin required a whole new kind of detective work made possible by the tools of modern molecular biology and genetics. In red light and then changes to the Pfr form. Conversely, when Pfr absorbs far red light it is converted back to the Pr form.

Phytochrome regulates a wide array of plant responses including seed germination, de-etiolation, synthesis of anthocyanin pigments in fruits such as apples, shoot elongation, leaf development, and flowering. Phytochrome is important to plants ecologically because it tells seeds whether or not they are in an appropriate situation for germination to proceed. Phytochrome also allows plants to sense whether they are in sun or shade and directs their development accordingly.

the 1980s, scientists working on phototropism in dark-grown seedlings discovered that blue light caused a phosphate group to be added to a particular protein, identified by its molecular mass of 120 kDa (Da = dalton. The dalton is defined as 1/12 of the mass of carbon 12). Cells to activate or "turn on" various proteins commonly use the addition of a phosphate group, or phosphorylation. They also found that the 120 kDa protein was localized in the actively growing regions of the seedlings: the same regions that responded most strongly to the phototropic stimulus.

A short time later, scientists in the same laboratory found a mutant in *Arabidopsis*, a common weed known as mouse-eared cress that has become a popular and productive research tool in plant laboratories around the world. This particular *Arabidopsis* mutant failed to respond to the phototropic stimulus and coincidentally lacked the 120 kDa protein. As expected, when the wild-type gene was isolated and cloned, it was shown to encode the 120 kDa protein. It was then relatively easy to show that the protein was actually a chromoprotein that contained riboflavin, a yellow pigment that absorbs blue light. The protein portion of the pigment molecule is responsible for the absorption in the ultraviolet. Because the pigment was responsible for absorbing the light that stimulated phototropism, it was given the name phototropin.

5 Photoperiodism and Biological Clocks

Morning is the best of all times in the garden. The sun is not yet hot. Sweet vapors rise from the earth. Night dew clings to the soil and makes plants glisten. Birds call to one another. Bees are already at work.

— William Longgood

Photoperiodism and Biological Clocks

TELLING TIME WITHOUT A WATCH

Over 250 years ago, Swedish botanist Carl von Linné, better known as Carolus Linnaeus, designed a floral clock based on the opening and closing of the floral petals at various times of the day. The flowers were arranged in a circle and one could tell the approximate time of day according to which flowers were open and which were closed. It may not have been the most accurate clock, but it does indicate that even that long ago, scientists recognized that plants are able to measure time.

GIANT TOBACCO AND SEPTEMBER SOYBEANS

In the early 1920s, two plant breeders, W.W. Garner and H.A. Allard, who worked with the United States Department of Agriculture, ran into a problem. Garner and Allard encountered a mutant tobacco plant (*Nicotiana tabacum*), called Maryland Mammoth, growing in their experimental plots near Washington, DC. The mammoth plants grew over 10 feet high but, much to the dismay of Garner and Allard, could not be used in breeding experiments because the plants never flowered in the field during the normal growing season. The Maryland Mammoth tobacco would only flower if cuttings were taken and grown in the greenhouse in the winter.

A second curious phenomenon was studied in the same laboratory: the flowering behavior of a particular variety of soybean (*Glycine max*). If successive plantings of Biloxi soybean were made over an 8- to 10-week period in the spring, all the plants flowered at roughly the same time in September. The oldest plants were 125 days old when they flowered and the youngest were only 58 days old. Clearly, age was not a significant factor in flowering. The plants, regardless of age, were all waiting for the same signal before flowering could begin.

In their experiments, Garner and Allard were able to eliminate a number of environmental conditions such as temperature, nutrition, and light intensity. They finally concluded, somewhat reluctantly, that flowering was controlled by day length, or **photoperiod**. They proceeded to describe the photoperiodic flowering behavior of scores of species and gave the phenomenon the name **photoperiodism**. At the time, Garner and Allard also suggested that bird migration might also be keyed to day length, a phenomenon that is now well documented. Indeed, we now know that photoperiodism is a key regulatory signal for many aspects of plant behavior, including tuber and bulb formation and autumn leaf drop of deciduous trees. Photoperiod also

From Railroad Carts to Biotrons

W. W. Garner and H. A. Allard concluded that photoperiod was responsible for the flowering behavior of Maryland Mammoth tobacco and Biloxi soybean. They also cataloged the photoperiodic behavior of many flowering species. To control day length, Garner and Allard devised a system of growing plants in pots placed on benches that road on rails like small railroad carts. The benches could then be rolled into darkened garage-like buildings at predetermined times near the end of the work day and returned to sunlight in the morning. It was a crude but effective system that allowed Garner and Allard to describe the photoperiodic responses of literally hundreds of plants over several years.

Today these same experiments would be conducted in much more sophisticated controlled environment chambers. Available in many sizes from small reach-in refrigerator-like chambers to giant walk-in cold rooms, the modern controlled environment chamber allows scientists to control the intensity, spectral distribution, and duration of light as well as temperature, humidity, nutrition, and other environmental parameters. Controlled environment chambers can provide instantaneous on-off lighting or be programmed to simulate sunrise and sunset. Entire buildings, called biotrons, are now being constructed with combinations of facilities that allow experiments on many plant interactions.

regulates mating behavior in a wide range of animal species. This discovery began with a tobacco mutant that was reluctant to accommodate the needs of plant breeders.

SHORT, LONG, AND NEUTRAL DAYS

The photoperiodic responses of plants can be conveniently grouped into one of three categories. The Maryland Mammoth tobacco and Biloxi soybean are both considered **short-day plants** (SDP) because they flower in response to short days. Other plants are considered **long-day plants** (LDP) because they flower in response to long days. Black henbane (*Hyoscyamus niger*), spring wheat (*Triticum aestivum*), and spinach (*Spinacea oleracea*) are typical long-day plants. The third category includes plants that flower regardless of photoperiod. These are called **day-neutral plants** (DNP). A lot of cultivated species such as corn (*Zea mays*), common bean (*Phaseolus vulgaris*), and sunflower (*Helianthus annus*) are day-neutral plants. In addition to these three basic response types, there are many other plants whose flowering behavior requires either a combination of short or long days. There are even some plants that flower on neither short days nor long days, but require an intermediate day length. The behavior of still others is modified by environmental conditions, usually temperature. We will have more to say about temperature and flowering in Chapter 6.

What is a short day and what is a long day? Consider the following example. The common cocklebur (*Xanthium strumarium*) is a short-day plant and black henbane is a long-day plant, yet both will flower when the day length is 12 to 13 hours. Thus it appears that *short day* and *long day* have nothing to do with absolute day length. Whether a plant is classified as a long-day plant or a short-day plant instead depends on its behavior relative to some **critical photoperiod** (Figure 5.1). A plant that flowers when the day length is *less than some maximum* (the **critical day length**) is classified as a short-day plant. A plant that flowers when the

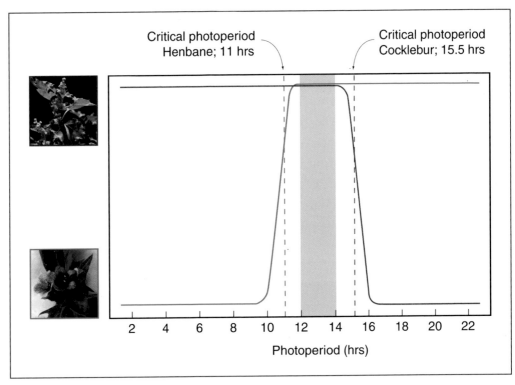

Figure 5.1 Critical photoperiod defines the flowering behavior of plants. Cocklebur is a short-day plant because it flowers when the photoperiod or day length is *shorter* than 15.5 hours. Henbane is a long-day plant because it flowers when the photoperiod or day length is *longer* than 11 hours.

day length is *greater than some minimum* (the critical day length) is classified as a long-day plant. The critical day length for the short-day plant cocklebur is 15.5 hours, meaning that it will flower whenever the day length is *shorter* than 15.5 hours. The critical day length for the long-day plant black henbane is 11 hours; it will flower when the day length is *longer* than 11 hours. Both will flower when the day length is 12 to 13 hours because this day length is shorter than the critical maximum for cocklebur and longer than the critical minimum for black henbane. The actual value of the critical day length varies widely from one species to the next.

As if to make it even more interesting, the concepts of photoperiod and critical *day length* apply only when the plants are growing on a normal 24-hour light-dark cycle. Suppose cockleburs were to be grown in a controlled environment chamber on a cycle with a periodicity other than 24 hours. What would happen, for example, on a 12-hour cycle with four hours of light followed by eight hours of darkness? You would expect cocklebur to flower because four hours of light is much less than the critical day length for cocklebur—but the plants will remain vegetative. Similarly, on a 48-hour cycle with 16 hours of light and 32 hours of darkness you would expect the plants to remain vegetative

Photoperiod and Floriculture

There are a number of economically important floricultural species that require specific day lengths (or night lengths) to flower. Chrysanthemums, poinsettias, and *Fuschia* are examples of flowers that are either available year-round (chrysanthemums, *Fuschia*) or at specific times of the year (poinsettias) because greenhouse growers have learned to manipulate photoperiod to control their time of flowering.

Chrysanthemums, a popular flower in bouquets and boutonnieres, are short-day plants that normally flower in the fall. When grown in the greenhouse, chrysanthemums will also flower in response to the short days of early spring. To bring chrysanthemums into flower during the long days of summer, the day length is shortened by covering the benches with a canopy of black cloth in late afternoon and withdrawing the cloth in the morning. In the fall and winter months, it may be necessary to extend the day length for a particular crop of chrysanthemums to prevent flowering until the flowers are needed for the market. Commercial growers in southern California do this in the field by hanging 100-watt bulbs about 2 m (6.5 ft) above the plants and 5.2 m (17 ft) apart. This arrangement does not provide a lot of light, but is sufficient to delay flowering.

because 16 hours of light is longer than its critical day length, but—you guessed it—the plants flower! Experiments like this tell us that plants do not measure the length of the light period. Plants actually measure the length of the *dark* period. Technically, the response might best be called **nyctiperiodism** but the term photoperiodism is well entrenched in the literature and so remains.

Now we can turn the definitions around and say that a short-day plant is actually a long night plant and a long-day plant is actually a short night plant. The critical day length for a short-day plant thus represents the maximum length of day *in a 24-hour period* that leaves a sufficiently long night to induce flowering.

Commercial growers extend day length and delay the flowering of poinsettias by using a similar arrangement of artificial lighting. Turning off the lights in October and covering the plants with black cloth will ensure a crop of brilliant red, white, or pink bracts 8 to 10 weeks later, just in time for the Christmas market.

Fuschia is a long-day plant native to tropical America. It is most commonly available in hanging baskets in floral shops. Commercial growers maintain stock plants for propagation under short-day conditions to prevent flowering and propagate them by vegetative cuttings. At the appropriate stage of growth, the young cuttings are induced to flower by exposing them to light for 4 hours in the middle of the night for three weeks. This treatment breaks up the long night, thus providing the equivalent of a long day. The plants can then be shipped off to the retail shop where they come in to flower about 4 weeks after the light treatment.

Understanding how to control flowering through manipulation of photoperiod has had a tremendous economic impact within the floriculture industry.

Conversely, the critical day length for a long-day plant is the minimum length of day in a 24-hour period that keeps the dark period short enough to allow flowering. For cocklebur, the critical dark period would be 8 to 9 hours (24 hrs minus 15.5 hrs) and for black henbane it would be 13 hours (24 hrs minus 11 hrs).

THE DARK PERIOD IS MEASURED IN THE LEAVES

When a plant switches from producing leaves to producing flowers, the change takes place in the shoot apical meristem. It would be natural to assume that the apex would also be the site that perceives the photoperiodic stimulus, but it is not. The role of the leaf can be shown very clearly with a plant such as cocklebur because a *single* dark period of sufficient length will set cocklebur plants irretrievably on the path toward flowering, even if the plant is otherwise maintained under long days. Not all plants will respond to a single inductive period—many require multiple inductive dark periods before significant flowering will occur. This capacity for floral induction with a single dark period is, incidentally, one reason why cocklebur has been a favorite plant for the study of photoperiodism.

With this in mind, we can do an interesting mind experiment. Assume that a group of cocklebur plants are maintained under long days. On each plant we will remove all but one leaf. Now we can expose either the apex *or* the remaining leaf to a long dark period simply by covering it with opaque black paper for more than eight hours. We then return the plants to long-day conditions and watch for flowering. The result will be that the plants on which the apex was given the short-day will remain vegetative while the plants on which the leaf was given the short-day will flower. This experiment tells us that the photoperiodic signal is perceived by the leaves.

We can add another interesting twist to this experiment. Cocklebur plants maintained on a regimen of 15 hours light and 9 hours darkness will flower. What do you think would happen if the cover were removed from the leaf halfway through the 9-hour dark period? The plant will remain vegetative because it has now experienced two 4-to-5-hour dark periods, both of which are less than the 8-to-9-hour critical dark period. Exposing the leaf to a single brief "light break" of 5 minutes is sufficient to prevent flowering. This, by the way, is another piece of evidence that confirms that plants measure the dark period because the opposite experiment, that is, interrupting a light period with a brief "dark break," has no effect. More important, however, is the observation that red light given during the light break is most effective at preventing flowering and the effectiveness of red light is reversible if followed immediately with far red light! This experiment confirms that phytochrome is involved in the photoperiodic response. We will return to the role of phytochrome in photoperiodism later in this chapter.

It is interesting to note that the sensitivity of cocklebur to induction by a single long dark period is not without its "dark side." In research greenhouses, experimental populations of cockleburs are maintained in the vegetative state by using artificial lighting to extend the day length, particularly in winter. A 16-to-17-hour day is sufficient to keep the plants non-flowering, but ready for flowering experiments. However, many an experiment has been ruined by a power failure that prematurely turns off the artificial lighting. The resulting single, long dark period will induce flowering in all of the plants and they must all be discarded. New plants must be sown and the experiments must start all over again.

THE ELUSIVE FLOWERING HORMONE

Now we know that the leaf detects the photoperiodic signal and that flowering occurs at the stem apex. Such a physical separation of detection and response raises the logical necessity of a floral stimulus formed in the leaves and transmitted from the leaf to the apical meristem. As early as 1936, the Russian plant physiologist M. Chailakhyan proposed that this stimulus was a flowering hormone that he named **florigen**. The existence of such a hormone was suggested by experiments in which several *Perilla* plants (SD plants) were grafted together in a series. A graft establishes continuity between the vascular tissues of grafted plants. If a plant at one end of a series is induced to flower with the proper photoperiod, all plants in the series will flower, even though the rest of the plants are maintained under photoperiods that are unfavorable for flowering. The results were interpreted to indicate that a flowering hormone was synthesized in the induced plant and that hormone was transported to the other plants in the line, causing them to flower. Unfortunately, all efforts over the past 70 years to isolate and identify florigen have been unsuccessful. The nature of the transmissible stimulus remains an elusive mystery even today.

Photoperiodism did not, of course, evolve for the benefit of plant breeders. The real significance of photoperiodism lies in synchronizing plant life cycles with the time of the year. Day length varies greatly with latitude and is the most predictable indicator of seasonal change (Figure 5.2). Photoperiodic control of flowering allows a species to flower and set seed within a particular temporal niche, which reduces competition with other species. Photoperiod also allows plants to *anticipate* the arrival of unfavorable climate. For some plants it ensures that seed formation can be completed before a killing frost. In temperate and northern latitudes, photoperiod is the signal that prepares maples and other deciduous trees to export nutrients from their leaves before dropping them in the fall. The recycled nutrients are stored in the trunks and roots over winter until required by the expanding buds the following spring.

THE INTERNAL CLOCK
One of the curious mysteries of plant behavior has long been the so-called sleep movements or **nyctinastic movements**, of leaves.

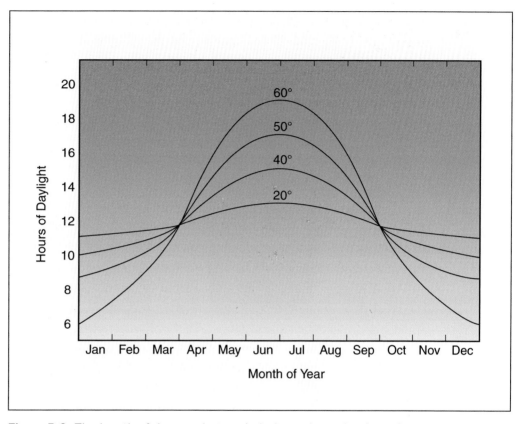

Figure 5.2 The length of day, or photoperiod, depends on the time of year and where you are with respect to the equator (0° latitude). This figure illustrates latitudes north of the equator. South of the equator, the curves would be offset by six months.

The leaves of many plants exhibit a periodic rise and fall over a 24-hour period. The primary (or first) leaves of the common bean, for example, rise to a horizontal position during the day and fall to a vertical position at night (Figure 5.3).

The mechanism for leaf movement is fairly well understood. At the point where the leaf blade joins the petiole is a bulbous structure called a **pulvinus**, which functions like a hinge. Certain cells in the pulvinus, called motor cells, either gain or lose water, depending on where they are located in the pulvinus. At night, motor cells on the upper side of the pulvinus take up water and

Figure 5.3 Bean leaves exhibit characteristic "sleep" movements. The leaves are (A) horizontal during daylight hours and (B) move to the vertical at night.

swell (or gain turgor) while corresponding cells on the lower side lose water and shrink. This causes the leaf to fold down to the vertical position. At dawn, the opposite occurs, with the upper cells shrinking and the lower cells swelling—the leaf then moves to the horizontal position.

At first glance, these movements appear to be driven by daily light/dark cycles much the same as photoperiodism or photosynthetic carbon uptake, for example. However, photosynthetic carbon uptake is periodic only because it is dependent on daylight and daylight is periodic over time. Photosynthesis is thus described as a **diurnal rhythm**, meaning that it is active only during the day. It can be shown, however, that the periodic oscillations of bean leaves and many other aspects of plant behavior are not dependent on external factors, which rules out photoperiodism and diurnal rhythms. Sleep movements and similar phenomena appear instead to be controlled by an internal time-measuring system known as the **biological clock**.

The biological clock was discovered by the German botanist Erwin Bünning in the 1920s. Bünning and his colleagues were interested in the periodic movement of bean leaves. They wanted

Did You Know?

Residents of northern Maine or Winnipeg, Canada, have fewer problems with hay fever than those who live south of latitude 45°N. Although the pollen of many different plants can bring on hay fever, the real culprit is common ragweed (*Ambrosia artemisifolia*). Ragweed is an annual SD plant with a critical photoperiod of about 14.5 hours. North of latitude 45°N the day length does not drop below 14.5 hours until sometime in August or later. This does not leave sufficient time for ragweed to flower and produce viable seed before the first killing frost. Consequently, ragweed is abundant only in more southern regions.

to avoid the influence of external factors such as light and temperature variations, so they set up their experiments in Bünning's potato cellar. They soon discovered that, in the constant conditions provided in the potato cellar, the leaf movement persisted. The rhythm of leaf movement persisted in the absence of any external cues, so it was concluded that the periodic rise and fall of the leaves was controlled by an internal or **endogenous** (Fr. *endogéne*, internal) timing mechanism that is now known as the biological clock.

The key to an endogenous rhythm is that it persists for at least several cycles under constant conditions, usually constant darkness. The time required to complete a single cycle is called the **period**, described as the time from peak to peak. In Bünning's experiment, the length of the period for leaf movement under a normal day/night regime was 24 hours, but when the plants were placed in continuous darkness the period was 25.4 hours. How do we account for this difference in periodicity? The period expressed under constant conditions is described as the **free-running period**. The free-running period is the natural period—free of external influence—of the endogenous clock. In the case of the bean leaves in Bünning's experiments, the free-running period was 25.4 hours. Under natural growing conditions, however, the period of bean leaf movements is 24 hours because they are *synchronized* to the solar day/night cycle (Figure 5.4). This synchronization is called **entrainment** and the signal that synchronizes the rhythm is commonly referred to as a **zeitgeber** (to give). Suppose you had an alarm clock that ran a little slow. Left unattended, the alarm would go off later and later each morning. You don't want to be late for your first class in the morning (and later each day), so every night when you go to bed you reset the clock to the actual time. Your alarm clock is a lot like the biological clock. It has a *free-running period* that is greater than 24 hours and when you reset it you are the *zeitgeber* that *entrains* the clock to a 24-hour period.

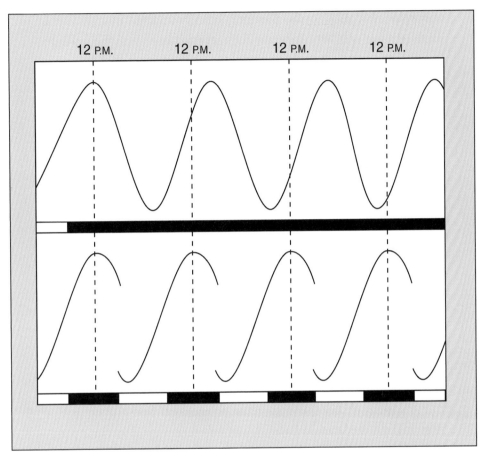

Figure 5.4 A free-running endogenous period of slightly more than 24 hours is synchronized to a 24-hour period by a light-on signal at dawn each day.

The signal that entrains bean leaf movement to a 24-hour cycle is the daily light-on signal, or dawn. Curiously, in their initial experiments Bünning and his colleagues found that the maximum night position of the bean leaves always occurred exactly 16 hours after their visits to the potato cellar. It turns out that this was because they used a very weak red light when watering their plants and tending their recording equipment. They assumed the red light was safe because at the time (the 1920s), phytochrome was unknown and there was no evidence that red light had any effect on plant morphogenesis. Bünning quickly realized that the weak red light was synchronizing the rhythm and only when the red light was eliminated was the free-running rhythm expressed. We now know that phytochrome, the red- and far red-light-absorbing pigment described in the previous chapter, has a prominent role in synchronizing endogenous rhythms!

Organisms are known to express a number of different rhythms that are classified according to the length of their free-running period. Bean leaf movement has a free-running period of *about* 24 hours and is thus classified as a **circadian rhythm** (*circa*, about; *dies*, day). Examples of circadian rhythms in plants include sleep movements in a large number of species, stomatal opening, stem growth, CO_2 production, changes in membrane potential, and the expression of messenger RNA. A **lunar rhythm** has a period of about 28 days, the time between one full moon and the next, and **annual rhythms** have a period of about one year. Lately, biochemists have become interested in rhythms in metabolic activity with periods measured in minutes or a few hours. These are known as **ultradian rhythms.**

A variety of experiments have established that the circadian clock is an important component of photoperiodic time measurement. Very young seedlings of the SDP lambs quarters (*Chenopodium rubrum*), for example, can be induced to flower with a single dark period presented during an otherwise continuous light regime. By varying the length of that single dark period, it can be shown that flowering behavior responds rhythmically with a free-running period of about 30 hours. In other words, a single dark period of 15 hours, 45 hours, *or* 75 hours will result in maximum flowering, but when the dark period is 30 hours or 60 hours, the plants do not flower.

ON THE TRAIL OF THE ENDOGENOUS CLOCK

Although it is relatively easy to demonstrate that a developmental event is under control of an endogenous clock, defining the nature and location of the clock is another problem entirely. Science moves forward primarily because the scientists asking the questions are able to control and manipulate events. This traditional approach does not work with the endogenous clock precisely because it is internal and, except for resetting by a light-on signal, does not respond to traditional methods of laboratory manipulation. Moreover, endogenous rhythms are fundamentally a question of time measurement, a concept that is difficult to imagine in terms of conventional cellular biochemistry.

One thing is clear—you would not expect to dissect a plant and find a watch with a quartz movement ticking away somewhere in a leaf or stem. But then when you look at a clock or wristwatch, you don't see the internal oscillator (a quartz movement, for example) either. All you see are the hands that tell you the time. In a similar way, developmental events such as leaf movement or flowering represent only the overt expression or "hands" of the endogenous biological clock. There must be a central oscillator, the oscillator is no doubt biochemical or genetic in nature, and it would likely be found within individual cells. Beyond that, little is really known about the clock.

A simple circadian system would have three components: input pathways, a central oscillator, and output pathways (Figure 5.5). The central oscillator is the primary timekeeper or clock that expresses a free-running periodicity under constant conditions. At least one input pathway would be phytochrome, which uses the light-on signal of dawn to continually "reset" the oscillator and keep it in phase with the ever-changing day/night cycle. The output pathways are clock-controlled genes.

Although none of the genes responsible for the clock itself have been identified, recombinant DNA and other modern techniques for exploring gene expression have led to the identification of several clock-associated genes. These are genes whose expression exhibits circadian oscillations and most of these genes that have been identified so far appear to encode proteins that

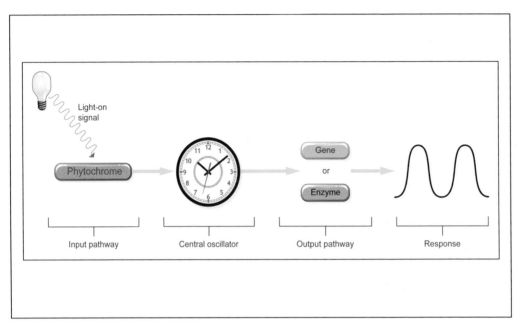

Figure 5.5 The key to the endogenous circadian clock is a central oscillator (or timekeeper), which may be a complex chemical reaction. The oscillator is regulated by input signals such as phytochrome. In turn, the oscillator regulates the periodic output of genes or enzymes to give the observed response.

are involved in photosynthesis. Photosynthesis does not operate at night, so there is no need for the cell to waste energy and carbon synthesizing large quantities of photosynthetic proteins that cannot be used at that time. These resources would be put to better use supporting other ongoing metabolic processes. But the biological clock is then able to tell the cell when it is time to start accumulating photosynthetic proteins that will be needed as daylight approaches. We can expect that more clock-associated genes will be discovered as this research progresses, eventually leading to identification of genes for the clock mechanism.

SUMMARY

The first firm indication that plants could measure time was the work by Garner and Allard, who discovered that plant flowering responses were controlled by day length, a phenomenon they called photoperiodism. Even though plants actually measure the length of a dark period, photoperiodic responses are classified as short-day, long-day, or day-neutral according to the plant's response to a critical photoperiod in a 24-hour regime. Short-day plants respond to a photoperiod shorter than some critical photoperiod, whereas long-day plants respond to a photoperiod longer than their critical photoperiod. Day-neutral plants, including most commercial crop species, flower irrespective of day length. The effects of interrupting the dark period with weak red and far red light have established that the light-on and light-off signals that determine the length of the dark period are sensed by phytochrome. Time measurement is a property of the leaves, which establishes the logical necessity for a transmissible stimulus, or hormone, that is translocated to the apex where vegetative development is turned off and floral development is turned on. The identity of the floral stimulus remains unknown.

Flowering is also one of many responses that are controlled by the endogenous, or internal, circadian biological clock. Circadian clocks express a periodicity of about, but not exactly, 24 hours under conditions such as constant darkness. Under a normal day/night regime, the clock is constantly reset to a 24-hour cycle by the light-on signal, or dawn. Although a number of clock-related genes have been identified, these are just the hands of the clock. The exact location and mechanism of the clock in plants remains a mystery.

6 Temperature and Development

To people who grumbled at the weather
he recommended a garden, "as the best of remedies
for that commonest of melancholies,"
for there is no weather that did not suit some plant.

— Liberty Hyde Bailey

Temperature and Development

In the introduction to their 1965 book *Light and Life,* H.H. Seliger and W.D. Glass observed, "The whole of nature is a trillion, trillion chemical machines. . . . " Whether one is speaking of chemistry in the chemist's domain or biochemistry in the biologist's domain, one thing is clear—plants, as chemical "machines," are universally sensitive to temperature. We often worry about temperature when we want to go on a picnic or skiing, but pay scant attention to the critical role that temperature plays in the lives of plants. Yet, along with water and light, temperature is one of the most critical factors in a plant's environment. At every level, whether that of an individual enzyme reaction, a metabolic sequence, or a complex physiological process, it is ultimately temperature that will determine whether or not the process can proceed and at what rate. Temperature has such an impact on biochemical reactions that it naturally plays a significant role in plant growth and development and, ultimately, the distribution of plants in space and time. In this chapter, we will examine the effect of temperature on growth in general. Some examples will illustrate how plants have learned to use temperature to direct some specific developmental events or adapt to their environment.

TEMPERATURE AND THE NATURAL ENVIRONMENT

Temperatures on earth range from the extremely hot in equatorial regions to extremely cold in polar and subpolar regions. Yet organisms of various shapes and sizes appear to inhabit all but a very few of the earth's habitats. The temperature at which biological reactions can occur is generally limited by the freezing point of water at the low end and the boiling point of water at the high end. The low end is limited by two factors; biochemical reactions will proceed very slowly at temperatures just above freezing and, much below freezing, ice crystal formation destroys the integrity of cells. At the high end, life is limited by the irreversible thermal denaturation (or destruction) of enzymes and other proteins.

It is generally believed that land plants probably first evolved in the tropics, not necessarily because of the warm temperatures, but because the temperature there was relatively stable. Plants gradually migrated into temperate regions both north and south of the equator only as they developed mechanisms that allowed them to accommodate wider variations in temperature on both a daily and a seasonal basis.

Organisms may be classified according to the temperatures at which they grow. Organisms that grow optimally at low temperatures (0°C to 10°C) are called **psychrophiles**. Psychrophiles include algae, fungi, and bacteria. Most higher plants are **mesophiles**, which means that they favor moderate temperatures and grow best between 10°C and 30°C. **Thermophiles** like it hot and grow best at temperatures between 30°C and 65°C, although there are reports of bacteria growing at temperatures as high as 85°C.

LOW TEMPERATURE CAN MODIFY FLOWERING BEHAVIOR

In many parts of North America, farmers plant wheat, rye, or barley in the fall. The seed germinates and sends out a few leaves and the seedlings then spend the winter under a blanket of snow. The seedlings resume growth in early spring after the snow has melted and the crop of grain is harvested usually about midsummer. Other plants such as cabbage, carrots, celery, Canterbury bells, and foxglove are biennials. They too survive over the winter and flower in their second season of growth. In both cases, the cold temperatures of the winter season have a direct role in the subsequent flowering behavior of the plants.

We will look at the cereal grains first. In most cereal grains, there are winter strains and spring strains (Figure 6.1). Spring strains are quantitative long-day plants (see Chapter 5). This means that under short days the plants will flower, but much later than under long days. For spring rye, for example, flowering under short days occurs only after 22 leaves have been

Figure 6.1 Cereal grains, such as wheat, oats, and rye, are grasses. The spring and winter strains respond differently to photoperiod and temperature.

produced, typically requiring about 4 to 5 months. Under long days, however, spring rye will flower after only seven leaves have been produced, requiring only 2 months. As the name suggests,

Wheat: The Stuff of Life

Wheat is one of the most ancient crops and was probably first cultivated by the Mesopotamians in the Fertile Crescent, an area of fertile land extending in an arc from Israel through present-day Iraq to the Persian Gulf. Today, wheat is grown almost everywhere in the United States and in central Canada except for New England and the Maritime provinces. Wheat accounts for 40% of cereal grain production worldwide.

In general, the severity of winter determines whether farmers plant winter wheat or spring wheat. Although winter wheat is able to acclimate to below freezing temperatures, if winter temperatures are too low or snow cover is inadequate, the seedlings may not survive. This is often the case in Montana, the Dakotas, and Minnesota, where spring strains are sown in the spring. In the central plains of Kansas, Nebraska, and Oklahoma, through Illinois and southern Ontario, the choice is winter strains that are sown in the fall.

Where it is possible to grow winter strains, they are preferred because of potentially higher yields. A spring strain has to be sown in the early spring when conditions may not be the best for seeding and germination; wet soils from melting snow may make it difficult to get machinery into the fields and may slow germination of the seed once it is sown. Winter strains are seeded in the fall when the soil is still warm and easily worked, so germination is rapid and the seedlings enter the winter with an established root system and three to five leaves. This means that when favorable weather returns in the spring, growth of the plant effectively picks up where it left off a few months before. The resulting head start gives winter strains a decided advantage—they flower and fill grain during mid-summer when photosynthetic potential is highest.

spring cereals are planted in the spring. They come into flower during the long days of mid-summer, and the grain is harvested in the fall. Winter cereals, on the other hand, are not normally sensitive to photoperiod and will take 4 to 5 months to flower regardless of day length. This means that winter strains planted in the spring do not flower early enough to produce mature grain before the first frosts occur in the fall. When subjected to an overwintering cold period, however, winter strains behave as quantitative long-day plants. They now respond to photoperiod, flower, and produce mature seeds just like the spring strains. The same effect can be achieved if germinated seeds of the winter strains are held near 1°C (34°F) for several weeks. Note that holding quiescent seeds at low temperature does not work. It is the meristem of an actively growing embryo that is sensitive, so the seed must be germinated before the low temperature will affect flowering behavior. Note also that the cold treatment does not promote flowering, but only renders the plant sensitive to photoperiod. This effect of temperature on photoperiodic behavior is called **vernalization**.

Biennial plants are another example where vernalization influences photoperiodic behavior. Cabbage, like most other biennials, grows in its first season as a rosette. Remember that the rosette habit is due to failure of internode elongation. The tight head of leaves surrounds the crown, or apical meristem, and protects it through the winter. When the meristem renews growth the following spring, it undergoes extensive stem elongation, a phenomenon called bolting, and flowers as a typical long-day plant. In the laboratory, holding young seedlings for 4 to 6 weeks at 5°C (41°F) can substitute for the overwintering treatment. The seedlings will skip the rosette stage, bolt, and flower.

Even though vernalization has been studied since the 1930s, the nature of the vernalized state remains somewhat of a mystery. It has been suggested that a transmissible stimulus, called vernalin, is involved. Unfortunately, vernalin has proven to be as elusive as the hypothetical flowering hormone, florigen. It was once suggested that vernalin could actually be the hormone gibberellin since it was observed that gibberellin can often substitute for the cold treatment. Spraying cabbage plants, for example, with a diluted solution of gibberellin at

Science and Politics

Vernalization is a translation of the Russian word *yarovizatsya*. Both words combine the root for spring (Russian, *yarov*; Latin; *vernalis*) with a suffix that means "to make," based on the observation that that a cold treatment "converts" the flowering behavior of a winter strain to that of a spring strain. The term vernalization was coined by Russian T.D. Lysenko in the 1920s and is probably the only physiological process of plants that has become entwined in political ideology.

Lysenko wrongly viewed vernalization as an *inheritable* conversion of the winter strain to the spring strain. This is a form of the Lamarckian theory of acquired characteristics. Jean-Baptiste Lamarck was a 19th century French naturalist who developed the theory that characteristics acquired during the lifetime of an organism could be inherited. For example, according to Lamarkism, repeatedly cutting the tails off mice would eventually lead to mice without tails. Lamarckism as a basis for evolution has, of course, been thoroughly discredited, but that didn't stop Lysenko's theory from eventually being officially sanctioned by the Marxist government of the Soviet Union. Many of the finest biologists in the Soviet Union refused to support the official line and were either demoted or simply disappeared.

The adoption of Lysenko's interpretation as the Soviet dogma in biology had a significant impact on Soviet biology and plant breeding, and placed agriculture in the Soviet Union at a severe disadvantage for several decades. It wasn't until N. Kruschev came to power in the 1950s that "Lysenkoism" was finally and officially buried.

normal temperatures will cause them to bolt and flower just as they do following a cold treatment. However, gibberellin is not vernalin, since gibberellin will promote flowering in *any* rosette plant whether or not it is one that normally requires a cold treatment. Any confusion between the roles of gibberellin and low temperature has been removed by recent genetic studies showing that vernalization and gibberellin act independently through separate genetic pathways.

THE DORMANCY OF BUDS IS SENSITIVE TO LOW TEMPERATURE

When temperate trees and shrubs renew their growth in the spring, the new growth arises from axillary buds that were formed the previous summer and survived over the winter. A bud is actually a meristem enclosed within a set of modified leaves called **bud scales** (Figure 6.2). The bud scales serve to insulate the bud and prevent it from drying out. At the same time that the leaves are shed in the fall, the buds will enter dormancy and they will not grow again until more favorable conditions return in the spring. Like seed dormancy, bud dormancy is characterized by low respiratory activity and the inability to grow even if temperature, oxygen, and water supply are adequate. Bud dormancy is an important defense mechanism, ensuring that the buds do not renew growth prematurely during an unseasonably warm spell in the middle of winter. Dormant buds require a minimum period at low temperature, usually 2 to 5 months at temperatures near or just above freezing, before dormancy is broken and renewed growth is possible.

TOPPING UP THE ANTIFREEZE TO SURVIVE WINTRY BLASTS

As late summer changes to fall, winter cereals and biennial rosettes as well as woody trees and shrubs are exposed to short days and gradually decreasing temperatures. These two stimuli— photoperiod and low, but above freezing, temperature—stimulate physiological modifications that enable the plants to survive

Figure 6.2 The overwintering buds of woody plants like this horse chestnut are enclosed within protective bud scales.

progressively lower temperatures. This process of change is referred to as **acclimation** and plants that have the capacity to acclimate to low temperatures are generally referred to as **winter hardy** or **freezing-tolerant**. Non-acclimated seedlings of winter rye (*Secale cereale*), for example, would normally be injured by temperatures just below freezing, but when fully acclimated will survive temperatures as low as -28°C (-18°F). Not surprisingly, trees and shrubs that inhabit north temperate, subarctic, and alpine regions are also able to acclimate to very low winter temperatures (Figure 6.3). A winter-hardy species of larch

Figure 6.3 Freezing-tolerant trees and shrubs in north temperate regions must acclimate to low temperatures every year in the autumn.

(*Laryx dihurica*), for example, lives in the most northernly forests of Siberia, where temperatures commonly reach -65°C (-85°F) in the dead of winter.

Curiously, it is not low temperature that causes low temperature injury in these plants—the damage is actually caused by the formation of ice crystals in the protoplast. We know this because dehydrated tissues such as seeds and fungal spores can withstand storage at temperatures close to absolute zero (0°Kelvin, or -273°C). Even fully hydrated, non-acclimated cells can survive immersion in liquid nitrogen (-196°C), but only if the rate of freezing is very rapid (greater than 100°C [212°F] per minute). Cells will survive very rapid freezing because the water freezes so quickly that it vitrifies (turns to glass); the water simply solidifies with no opportunity for ice crystals to form. On the other hand, not even a fully acclimated winter-hardy species can survive the formation of ice crystals in the protoplast. Once ice crystals form inside the protoplast, death invariably results. In nature, the temperature at which ice crystals form in the protoplasts determines the minimum survival temperature, and consequently the geographical distribution, of acclimated species.

The progress of ice crystal formation and protection from freezing damage has been studied most extensively in overwintering herbaceous plants such as winter wheat, winter rye, and spinach. As the ambient temperature falls below freezing, ice first forms *outside* the cells in the intercellular spaces collectively referred to as the **apoplast**, including the spaces within the network of cellulose fibers in the cell walls, in the corners where adjacent cells meet, and in the hollow water-conducting elements called xylem vessels. Ice forms here first because this is where water is the purest. This extracellular ice formation does not injure the cells, but ice crystals grow by adding water molecules. So as the ice crystals grow, the extracellular water consumed in their formation is replaced by water migrating out of the protoplast. Extracellular ice formation thus leads eventually to desiccation of the protoplasm, which in turn causes a loss of enzyme activity and disruption of cellular membranes.

Plants thus face two challenges when preparing for survival at low temperatures: (1) how to prevent extracellular ice crystal formation and the resulting desiccation of protoplasm and (2) how to prevent ice crystal formation in the protoplasts. Both challenges are met by synthesizing new proteins. During acclimation, whole new sets of cold-regulated genes are activated. The products of these genes include two new classes of proteins called **antifreeze proteins** and **cryoprotective proteins.**

Antifreeze proteins were first discovered in cold water fish but have recently been discovered in winter annual and biennial plants. They are small proteins that are secreted into the apoplast of the leaves and crown (the apical mersitem). Here they bind onto the surface of the ice crystals and prevent further growth. The function of antifreeze proteins thus appears to be to suppress extracellular ice crystal formation which, in turn, prevents desiccation of the protoplast.

Cryogenic Storage

Storage in liquid nitrogen, known as **cryogenic storage**, is commonly used to preserve sperm cells for later use in artificial insemination of horses, cattle, and humans. It is also used for long-term storage of fungi, other microorganisms, and tissue samples. Immersion of small samples contained in glass "straws" in the very cold liquid nitrogen (-196°C, or -321°F) freezes the samples rapidly enough that ice crystals cannot form. When retrieving samples from cryogenic storage, however, it is necessary to thaw the material equally rapidly to avoid ice nucleation and crystal growth as the sample returns to room temperature. You can perhaps understand why attempts to preserve human beings with the hope of later bringing them back to life are considered science fiction. There is simply no way the temperature in such a dense tissue mass could be lowered (or raised) rapidly enough to prevent ice crystal formation and irreversible cell damage.

Cryoprotective proteins are also small proteins but they are retained within the cell where they help to prevent freezing of the protoplast. These proteins are very **hydrophilic** (water-loving), which means they have a very high affinity for water. By binding so much water, the cryoprotective proteins prevent the protoplasmic water from forming ice crystals. Cryoprotective proteins also interact with other proteins and membranes in the cell in a way that enhances their stability at freezing temperatures.

THERMOPERIODISM AND THERMONASTY

For a long time, growers have recognized that many plants grow better when grown under alternating day/night temperature regimens. Tomatoes, for example, grow poorly when grown at constant temperatures of 26°C (79°F) or 18°C (64°F), but with daytime temperatures of 26°C and nighttime temperatures of 18°C the plants grow vigorously and produce the maximum amount of fruit. This type of response to alternating temperatures is known as **thermoperiodism**. Unlike photoperiodism, which affects mostly flowering behavior, thermoperiodism influences primarily vegetative growth.

Alternating temperatures also influence floral movements in certain groups of plants. This is particularly true of members of the family Liliaceae, including tulips and crocus (Figure 6.4). Flowers of tulip and crocus are normally open during the daylight hours and closed at night. You might expect that these movements are regulated by light, but it is actually a response to changing temperatures and involves differential growth on the inner and outer surfaces of the perianth segments (in the Liliaceae the sepals and petals are indistinguishable; see Chapter 7). Such a temperature-dependent growth response is known as **thermonasty**. The flowers open in response to an increase in temperature because of a relative increase in the growth rate of cells on the inner surface of perianth parts, whereas closure following

Figure 6.4 The petals on tulip flowers open as the temperature increases and close as the temperature decreases.

a drop in temperature appears to be caused by a transient increase in the growth of cells on the outer surface. A large temperature change is not required; a change of a few degrees is sufficient to bring about either opening or closure. There are lower limits, however, and if the days are very cold both tulips and crocuses will remain closed during the daylight hours.

SURVIVING HIGH TEMPERATURES

In desert areas, plants are commonly exposed to extremes of high temperature. Both low temperatures and high temperatures represent environmental stress to plants. Plants that survive low temperature undergo physiological changes that allow them to acclimate to the stress. Plants rarely acclimate to high temperatures, rather they adapt. The difference between acclimation and **adaptation** is significant. Acclimation refers to non-heritable physiological modifications that occur, perhaps repeatedly, over the lifetime of an individual. Adaptation refers to heritable changes in structure or function that increase the fitness of a particular organism for a particular environment.

The primary stress that plants face under low temperatures is ice crystal formation, and plants acclimate or deal with this stress by synthesizing antifreeze or cryoprotectant proteins that prevent ice crystal formation. The primary stress in a high temperature environment, however, is excess water loss or desiccation. Without special protection, desert plants would simply dry out! Most plants adapt by minimizing water loss or avoiding it altogether. Ephemeral plants, for example, germinate, grow, and flower very quickly following seasonal rains. They avoid high temperature stress by completing their life cycle during non-stressful periods. **Succulent plants** are plants that have heavy cuticles covering thick, fleshy leaves. Succulents avoid high temperature stress by reflecting light from their shiny leaves and storing large quantities of water. The cacti are an extreme example of succulent plants (Figure 6.5). The leaves of cacti are reduced to thorns. Their upright orientation reduces thermal load by minimizing heat absorption and they store large quantities of water in their fleshy stems.

Figure 6.5 The structure of succulent plants like these cacti is designed to minimize heat load and conserve water.

There are relatively few perennial herbaceous plants in desert regions and those that do occur there are often dormant for much of the year. Leaves of desert plants are often oriented in such a way to minimize heat absorption. Finally, many desert plants have modified photosynthetic mechanisms with higher optimum temperatures or the capacity to conduct photosynthesis while minimizing water loss through the leaves.

SUMMARY

The growth and development of a plant is the summation of trillions of biochemical reactions that are sensitive to temperature. Temperature is a critical factor in a plant's environment and may play a significant part in growth and development. Plant life is generally limited by the freezing point of water at the low end of the temperature scale and the irreversible denaturation of proteins at the high end.

Low temperature has specific effects on the flowering behavior of plants, especially with respect to winter cereals and biennials, a phenomenon known as vernalization. Unvernalized winter cereals do not respond to photoperiod, whereas vernalized winter cereals behave as quantitative long-day plants. Biennials typically grow in a rosette habit during the first year but undergo extensive stem elongation and behave as long-day plants after vernalization. Buds on woody trees and shrubs in north-temperate, artic, and alpine regions go dormant in the fall and will not break dormancy until after a prolonged cold treatment. Woody species in northern latitudes also acclimate to low winter temperatures by synthesizing antifreeze and cryoprotectant proteins that protect the cells and tissues against damage by ice crystal formation.

Plants growing in high temperature environments, such as those typically encountered in deserts, face the constant prospect of excessive water loss. Such plants do not generally acclimate to high temperature but have evolved heritable adaptations to avoid or reduce the impact of water stress.

7 Flowers and Fruits

The flower is the poetry of reproduction.
It is an example of the eternal seductiveness of life.

— Jean Giraudoux,
The Enchanted, 1933

Flowers and Fruits

A FLOWER IS MORE THAN JUST A PRETTY FACE

Most people are generally attracted to plants—flowering plants in particular. The natural beauty of flowers graces all aspects of our lives. Psychologists tell us we are attracted to flowers because they are restful and evoke a sense of well-being. We anticipate the arrival of crocuses and daffodils as the first signs of spring, provide corsages and boutonnieres for our dates, and mark special occasions such as weddings and funerals with flowers. Flowers also provide many of the fruits and vegetables that humans and other animals consume for nutrition.

The flower is also a solution to several major evolutionary problems faced by plants. In primitive plants such as algae, mosses, and ferns, sexual reproduction requires that a naked, mobile sperm swim through water to reach the egg. As plants developed vascular systems and elongated stems moved a significant portion of the plant into the hostile aerial environment, their reproductive structures could no longer depend on the availability of free water for bringing together the male and female gametes. The naked sperm was replaced with pollen grains that could be transferred to the female organs by wind or other vectors. First came the conifers or gymnosperms, but their seeds lay naked on cone scales and only random currents of wind could disseminate pollen. By contrast, flowering plants developed brightly colored petals to attract insects, birds, and mechanisms to engage these animals, unwittingly at times, in the transfer of pollen directly from the male organ of one plant to the female organ of another. In flowering plants, the seed was also encased in a fruit that provided protection and assisted in the dissemination of seeds over a wider geographical area.

ALL FLOWERS FOLLOW A COMMON PLAN

In spite of the enormous range of shapes, colors, and sizes in flowers, all flowers are constructed along a common theme

116

(see Figure 1.2). The flower is supported by a flower stalk, which is called the **pedicel** (if it supports a solitary flower) or **peduncle** (if it supports one flower in a group or inflorescence). The upper part of the stalk to which the floral appendages are attached is called the **receptacle**. The lowermost floral appendages are **sepals** and **petals**. Sepals and petals are the most leaf-like of the floral structures. Sepals and petals are also sterile appendages in the sense that, although they attract pollinators, they are not directly involved in the reproductive process. Sepals—collectively called the **calyx**—are commonly green or brown and most often serve as the structures that cover the flower bud before it opens. The petals—collectively called the **corolla**—are usually brightly colored and serve primarily to attract insects, birds, and other pollinators—not to mention gardeners. In some flowers, such as lilies for example, the sepals are also brightly colored and indistinguishable from the petals.

The stamens—collectively called the **androecium** ("house of man")—are the male reproductive structures. In most angiosperms the stamen consists of a two-lobed **anther** borne upon a slender stalk or filament, which is essentially a modified leaf midrib. The anther is the organ that produces pollen.

The centrally-located **carpels**—collectively called the **gynoecium** ("house of woman")—contain the ovules, or eggs, which develop into seeds after fertilization (Figure 7.1). Carpels are the distinctive feature that sets the angiosperms or flowering plants apart from all other plants. The word angiosperm is derived from the Greek words *angeion*, or vessel, and *sperma*, seed; the carpel is the floral "vessel" in which the seeds are produced. Most flowers contain carpels that fuse to form a **pistil** (Figure 7.2). The pistil consists of three parts—the **stigma**, **style**, and **ovary**. The stigma, at the top of the pistil, is a receptive surface that collects pollen. The stigma is a glandular tissue that secretes a sugary solution. The sticky sugar helps to trap the pollen and facilitates the germination and subsequent growth of the pollen after it lands.

The style is simply a region of the pistil that separates the stigma from the ovary and provides a channel for the pollen tube as it grows towards the ovary.

At the base of the pistil is the ovary. The ovary contains the eggs and is the part of the flower where the seeds are produced. Ovaries may be either superior or inferior, depending on where the sepals, petals, and stamens are attached. If the sepals, petals,

Supermarket Botany

You can learn a lot about plants just by examining fruits and vegetables available in the local supermarket. Take the business of carpels and fruits, for example.

Most ovaries in most pistils consist of two or more fused carpels. The ovary is thus divided into a corresponding number of chambers or locules in which the ovules, and eventually the seeds, are found. This can be seen by slicing an apple in half across, not length-wise. In the center (or core) you will see a five-pointed star. Each arm of the star represents one locule or carpel in cross section. Note that there are five carpels. The apple is in the genus *Malus* of the Rosaceae or rose family, which is characterized by having floral parts in fives: five sepals, five petals, and five carpels. Also, each locule contains a number of seeds, which tells you that each carpel had numerous ovules.

The fleshy part of the apple, the part that you eat, is actually the receptacle. Like the ovary wall in other fruits, the receptacle has undergone extensive growth following pollination due to the influence of hormones, primarily auxins, originating in the developing seeds. The sweet fleshy fruit is actually a ruse to entice animals such as humans to aid in the dispersal of the species. You are expected to discard the seeds some distance from the parent plant after you have consumed the flesh.

Examine other fruits (and vegetables) like peppers, tomatoes, and so forth to see if you can identify the carpels.

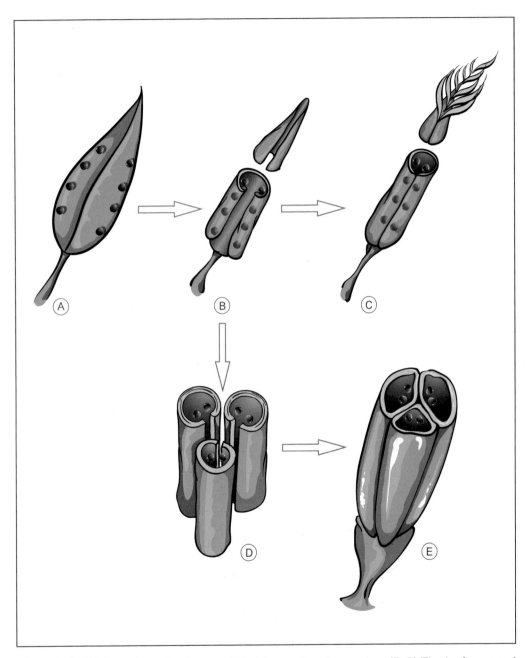

Figure 7.1 (A) Carpels evolved as modified leaves bearing ovules. (B-C) The leaf wrapped inward and formed a cap, which protected the carpels. With time, (D) multiple carpels fused to form (E) the pistil.

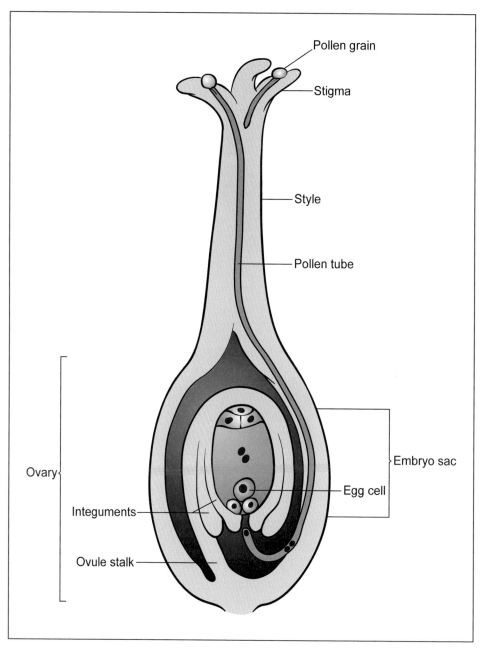

Figure 7.2 The embryo sac contains the egg cell that is fertilized by a male nucleus delivered by the pollen tube. A single pistil may contain hundreds of embryo sacs, each producing one seed.

and stamens are attached to the receptacle below the ovary, the ovary is considered **superior**. If the sepals, petals, and stamens appear to be attached to the top of the ovary, the ovary is considered **inferior** (Figure 7.3). In the case of an inferior ovary, the ovary is actually contained within the receptacle. The ovary and, in some cases, the receptacle have an important role in fruit development.

FROM LEAVES TO FLOWERS

A vegetative meristem is an indeterminate shoot. Indeterminate means that the meristem continually renews itself while producing a potentially unlimited succession of leaves and branches. When the flowering signal reaches a vegetative apical meristem, that meristem switches over from the production of leaf primordia to the production of floral parts and becomes a determinate shoot. A floral meristem is limited to only four whorls—sepals, petals, stamens, and carpels, in that order. Looking at a rose or an iris flower, it may be difficult to picture the floral structures as leaves but in developmental terms, all four of the floral appendages are considered modified leaves.

The conversion of a vegetative meristem to a floral meristem is a pretty dramatic change. How does it all come about? We do not know what kind of signal is produced in the leaves, but we know that when it reaches the meristem it induces a change in gene expression—vegetative, or leaf-encoding, genes are turned off and flowering genes are turned on. The first set of genes involved determines when and how the apex is susceptible to the floral stimulus—these are called **flowering-time genes**. Flowering-time genes determine whether the apex is susceptible to the floral stimulus that arrives from the leaves. In some plants the flowering-time genes are turned on early in the life history of the plant. Japanese morning glory (*Pharbitis nil*), for example, can be induced to flower as soon as the cotyledons have

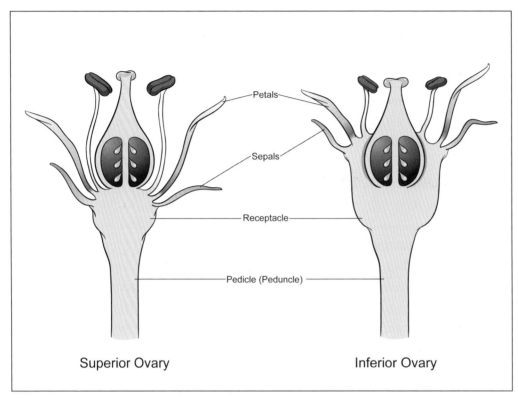

Superior Ovary   Inferior Ovary

Figure 7.3 An ovary may be superior or inferior depending on its position relative to the attachment of other floral parts. Tulip and lily flowers have superior ovaries. Cherry and apple flowers are examples of inferior ovaries.

expanded. In other cases, the plant must pass through a juvenile phase before the flowering-time genes are turned on and the apex is receptive to the floral stimulus. European beech (*Fagus sylvatica*), for example, has a juvenile phase that lasts 30 to 40 years.

The second set of genes is known as **floral-identity genes**. Floral-identity genes are turned on by the flowering-time genes. Floral-identity genes commit the meristem to the production of floral primordia rather than leaf primordia. The floral-identity genes in turn activate the third set, or **organ-identity genes,** that control the progressive development of sepals, petals, stamens, and pistils.

POLLEN AND EGGS

Pollen is produced when a diploid **microspore mother cell** in the anther divides by meiosis. Remember that a diploid cell has two copies of each chromosome and that meiosis is a reduction division. The result is four haploid cells. Each haploid cell becomes a pollen grain with one copy of each chromosome. A further division produces two haploid nuclei in each pollen grain. The pollen grains then develop a thick outer wall, or **exine**, that is often highly sculptured and contains numerous pores. Pollen grains vary considerably from one species to the next in their size, shape, the number and arrangement of pores, and sculptured exine. Many species of plants can be identified solely on the characteristics of their pollen grains. Due to the high chemical resistance of the exine, pollen is also well represented in the fossil record. These two factors—uniquely sculptured walls and resistance to decay—combine to provide a valuable record of plant history and, by implication, the climate that may have prevailed in the past.

Meanwhile, in the ovary, a diploid **megaspore mother cell** undergoes meiosis to produce four haploid daughter nuclei. Three of these nuclei usually disintegrate and the fourth divides by mitosis three times to produce eight nuclei. One of these nuclei becomes separated from the others by a wall to form an egg cell. Two of the nuclei, called polar nuclei, migrate to the center and form a large binucleate central cell. The other five nuclei are walled off to form small cells that serve relatively minor roles. All seven cells form what is now called the **embryo sac** (see Figure 7.2). The embryo sac is enclosed within two layers of maternal protective cells called **integuments**.

POLLINATION AND FERTILIZATION

A flower is able to fulfill its function of seed production only if pollen from the anther is first transferred to the stigma of a pistil and then able to deliver the sperm nucleus to the egg cell. This transfer of pollen to the surface of the stigma is called **pollination.**

Some flowers are self-pollinated, which means that the pollen need only travel a short distance between the anther and the stigma within the same flower. This is a relatively simple mechanism, but self-pollination does preclude genetic re-assortment and ensures that the offspring are genetically identical. Self-pollination is not possible in many plants for a variety of reasons. For example, in the same flower, the pollen and pistil may not mature at the same time, or the pollen may be unable to fertilize a pistil in the same flower (called **self-incompatibility**), or the plant may have separate male and female flowers.

Plants that are not capable of self-pollination must be **cross-pollinated**; pollen from one plant must be carried to the flower of another plant. The most obvious mechanism for cross-pollination is for the pollen to be carried by wind or, in the case of aquatic plants, water. Most grasses, including cereal grains, and most forest trees such as oaks, maples, and birches are wind pollinated. Wind-borne pollen, especially from the ragweed plant (*Ambrosia*), is the common cause of "hay fever" allergies. The allergic reactions are caused by proteins located in the outer wall of the pollen grain. The most intriguing pollination mechanisms involve insects, birds, and other animals. Flowers have developed an amazing array of modifications to attract animal vectors and entice them to carry pollen from one flower to the next. However, that is another story for another time. Here we are more concerned with what happens once the pollen grain arrives on the stigma of a pistil, regardless of how it got there.

Pollen shed from an anther is dry, so the first thing a pollen grain does when it lands on the stigma is take up additional water. It then produces a tube that emerges through one of the pores in the exine and grows down into the style. This is called germination. Of the two haploid pollen nuclei, one (called the

tube nucleus) leads the way down the tube as the tube elongates. The other nucleus divides to produce two sperm nuclei. When the tube reaches the ovary it breaches the wall of the embryo sac and releases the two sperm nuclei. Ultimately, one of the sperm nuclei enters the egg cell and fuses with the egg cell nucleus to form a diploid zygote. The second sperm nucleus migrates to the central cell where it fuses with the two polar nuclei. The involvement of two sperm in this way is called **double fertilization**, a process that is unique to sexual development in the angiosperms. Incidentally, in ovaries that produce many seeds—in some ovaries the seeds may number in the hundreds—a separate pollen grain and pollen tube is required for each seed that forms.

Once fertilization has been completed, the zygote then proceeds to develop as the embryo, the triploid nucleus divides to form the endosperm, and the integuments will eventually form the seed coat. Here we are back at the seed, which is where we started.

POSTSCRIPT: FROM FLOWERS TO FRUIT

Although we have now completed the cycle from seed to seed, plant development does not end. As the ovules develop into seeds, the surrounding ovary wall or **pericarp** develops into a fruit. Although the botanical definition of a fruit is relatively simple—a ripened ovary wall and its contents (seeds included)—there is an almost infinite range of fruiting structures. Fruit thus includes the usual apples, peaches, pears and watermelons, but also tomatoes, beans, cucumbers, and a variety of other foods that you might normally consider vegetables. The acorn is also a fruit, although in this case the pericarp is dry and hard.

Fruits derived from a single pistil or ovary (citrus, apples, peas, beans, etc) are considered **simple fruits. Aggregate fruits,** such as blackberries and raspberries, are derived from fused multiple ovaries. Citrus fruits and apples are also classified as fleshy fruits, whereas peas and beans are classified as dry fruits. Both the peel and the juicy part of an orange are derived from the ovary wall. In a fruit like an apple, the ovary wall is simply the membranous material that surrounds the core. An apple flower has an inferior ovary and the edible flesh of an apple is derived from the receptacle. Then there are problems such as nuts; hazelnuts and acorns, for example, are true nuts (meaning they have a woody pericarp) but the peanut is a bean, not a nut.

In most circumstances, a fruit will not develop unless pollination and fertilization have occurred. The primary signal for

Did You Know?

Do you know what plant produces the largest fruit? At fall fairs and other rural gatherings across North America, farmers and backyard gardeners compete every year to see who can grow the largest pumpkin. Contestants must carefully prepare the soil, select their best seeds, and time the germination and transplanting of the seedlings just right. Fertilization and watering schedules are critical if your pumpkin is to end up on the podium. Most growers use a strain of seed called Atlantic Giant, originally selected by Howard Dill of Nova Scotia. Al Eaton of Richmond, Ontario, whose 2004 effort topped out at 1,446 pounds, holds the current world record. That is a lot of pumpkin pies, but no doubt larger pumpkins will weigh more in future years.

Remember that the giant pumpkin, like any other fruit, gets all of its water and nutrients from the parent plant. If it takes about 100 days from pollination to harvest (and, of course, judging), the parent plant needed to supply Mr. Eaton's winning pumpkin with an average of 14 pounds of water and sugars each day, and all of that had to move through the relatively small core of vascular tissue in the stem that attached the pumpkin to the vine.

setting fruits appears to be hormonal—most likely auxin but cytokinins and gibberellins may also be involved. We know that auxin is important because both pollen and developing seeds are sources of auxin and experiments have shown that auxin has a significant role in fruit set and development. In many species, pollination alone is sufficient to stimulate fruit set. Experiments conducted in the 1930s showed that pollen was a rich source of auxin and that fruit set in tomatoes and other plants of the family Solanaceae could be induced by treatment with pollen extracts that contain auxin.

Strawberries provide a nice experimental system in which to test the hormone theory because the seeds (which are actually individual fruits called achenes) are borne on the surface and are easily removed. The "fruit" that you enjoy on your ice cream every spring is actually the fleshy receptacle. In a classic experiment, French botanist J. P. Nitsch found that removal of the developing achenes from a young strawberry prevented development of the fleshy receptacle. If the receptacle was treated with auxin after the achenes were removed, a normal strawberry fruit developed.

The development of a fruit takes place in three stages: maturation, ripening, and senescence. Maturation begins at the early stages and ends when the fruit achieves full size. Initially—up to perhaps the first 30 days in large fruits—growth is largely by cell division. As maturation progresses, the cells enlarge, the fruits accumulate carbohydrates and other flavor components, and the amount of acidity decreases.

Ripening begins after full maturation with a softening of the fruit flesh, development of characteristic flavors, and an increase in the amount of fluid components, or juice. As a result of these changes, the fruit becomes more visible and palatable and thus attractive to animals that eat the fruit and scatter the seed. A fruit softens during the ripening stage due to increased activity of pectinase, an enzyme that breaks down pectin. Pectin is a carbohydrate that glues the cells together. When pectin is degraded, the bonds between the cells are weakened and the fruit softens. Pectin is also the substance that makes a fruit jelly "gel." Overly ripe fruits tend to make a jelly with lots of flavor, but do not gel as well as jellies made with mature or only slightly ripe fruits. That is because overly ripe fruits contain less pectin. In the kitchen, of course, the solution is to add commercially prepared pectin. Check the ingredients label on the jar when you spread jam on your toast in the morning—it will probably include pectin.

Ripening can occur either before or after picking. When fruits must be shipped over long distances, it is common practice to pick them when mature but not fully ripe. They continue to ripen in transit and are intended to arrive at the market in peak condition. Ripening is stimulated by the plant hormone ethylene, which is given off by the fruit. However, the ripening process can be helped along, as is often the case with bananas, tomatoes, and some other fruits. Bananas are picked and shipped green. On arrival at the wholesale distributor, the bananas are placed in an airtight room which is then filled with ethylene gas. Twenty-four to 48 hours later, the bananas are removed from the room and shipped to the retail market where they turn yellow over the next few days.

During ripening, one of the characteristic changes is a gradual decrease in the respiratory rate in fruits. However, in some fruits there occurs a very abrupt reversal with the respiration rate rising as the fruit ripens, finally reaching a peak and then a decline. This abrupt change in respiratory rate is called the **climacteric**. Apples, pears, peaches, bananas, and avocados are examples of climacteric fruits. Cherries, citrus, pineapples, and grapes are examples of non-climacteric fruits that do not exhibit the respiratory rise. The climacteric is of some concern commercially because it is accompanied by the evolution of unusually high amounts of ethylene. Ethylene production at this stage stimulates the onset of senescence or the rapid aging and, ultimately, the general degradation of the fruit. This is why the one rotten apple can cause the others in the barrel to spoil.

Ripening in climacteric fruits is controlled by storing the fruit under controlled atmospheric conditions. Controlled atmospheric conditions include lowering oxygen levels (down to 1% from 21%), increasing carbon dioxide levels (up to 1% or more from the normal 0.03%), and decreasing temperature. These conditions reduce respiration rate, largely prevent the climacteric rise, delay the climacteric-associated release of ethylene,

Fruit Ripening and Biotechnology

Tomatoes are a difficult fruit to market because they tend to ripen and senesce relatively quickly. Tomatoes have a short shelf life. Back in the 1980s, a small biotech company in California found a way to delay the softening of tomatoes in order to extend their shelf life. They achieved this by isolating and cloning the gene for pectinase, the enzyme that degrades the pectin that holds the cells together. They then reinserted the gene in the tomato the "wrong" way. In the same way that you would have difficulty reading this sentence if it were inverted on the page, the cell was unable to read the inverted pectinase gene. As a result, tomatoes carrying the inverted gene produced much less pectinase. This meant that the fruit could be left longer on the vine in order to develop color and flavor constituents, which proceeded normally and yet remained firm.

This engineered tomato, called Flavr-Savr™, was the first genetically engineered organism to be released for commercial production. The Flavr-Savr™ tomato, however, was eventually pulled from the market; not because of any genetic engineering controversy, but because the young company, while strong on science, was weak in the areas of crop production, marketing, and distribution.

and enable growers to store fruit like apples for months without losing quality.

Some fruits such as navel oranges, some bananas, Oriental persimmon, many fig cultivars, and some grapes are known to ripen spontaneously, even in the absence of fertilization of the egg. This is known as **parthenocarpy**. Without fertilization, of course, no seeds can be formed, so parthenocarpic fruits are seedless.

SUMMARY

The flower represents a major evolutionary advance as indicated by the number of flowering plant species; there are more species of angiosperms than any other group of plants. The flower allows for pollen vectors other than water and wind, which means the angiosperms have been able to exploit a wider variety of ecological niches.

In spite of the enormous variety in size and shape of flowers, all flowers follow the same basic plant of four whorls of appendages: sepals, petals, stamens, and pistils. The pistil is derived from carpels, the singular distinctive feature that sets angiosperms apart from all other plants. The carpel contains the ovules and is the site of fertilization and seed formation.

Conversion of the vegetative apex to a floral apex involves at least three sets of genes: genes that determine the receptivity of the apex to the floral signal that is sent from the leaves, genes that program the switch from leaf production to production of floral structures, and genes that determine the progressive development of sepals, petals, stamens, and pistils.

Pollination occurs when a pollen grain lands on a receptive stigmatic surface, germinates, and sends out a pollen tube that carries two sperm nuclei through the style to the ovary. Angiosperms are characterized by double fertilization; one sperm nucleus fertilizes the egg cell which develops into the embryo while the second sperm nucleus fertilizes the two polar nuclei to form the nutrient-rich endosperm.

As the seed develops, the surrounding ovary wall (sometimes including the receptacle) develops into a fruit. Fruit ripening is stimulated by ethylene. Controlled environment storage of fruit is designed to suppress respiration and ethylene production and consequently delay ripening. Seedless fruits will be produced when the fruit develops spontaneously in the absence of fertilization.

Glossary

Abscisic acid—A plant hormone that is involved primarily in signaling soil water deficits.

Abscission—The dropping off of leaves, fruits, and other plant organs.

Acclimation—Physiological changes that prepare an individual organism for adverse conditions or stress.

Adaptation—A heritable characteristic that improves the fitness of an organism for its environment.

Adventitious roots—Roots that arise in places where roots are not normally expected, such as cut stems or leaves.

After-ripening—Metabolic changes that must occur in some seeds after they are shed but before they will germinate.

Aggregate fruit—A fruit formed of multiple carpels within a single flower, such as raspberries or blackberries.

Androecium—The floral whorl containing the stamens or male reproductive organs.

Angiosperms—The group of plants whose seeds are borne within a mature ovary; the flowering plants.

Annual rhythms—A rhythm with a cycle time of about one year.

Anther—The terminal portion of the stamen in which pollen is produced.

Antifreeze proteins—Proteins that prevent ice crystal formation in the extracellular spaces.

Apical dominance—The suppression of lateral bud development under the influence of an apical bud.

Apical meristem—The growing point at the tip of a root or shoot.

Apoplast—The water-filled extracellular continuum of a plant. The apoplast consists of intercellular spaces, cell wall spaces, and water-filled xylem vessels.

Auxin—A plant hormone that controls cell enlargement and other effects.

Bark—A non-technical term applied to everything outside the vascular cambium in a woody stem or root.

Biological clock—The internal timing mechanism that regulates endogenous rhythms.

Biotron—A complex of growth chambers, greenhouses, and other facilities for studying plant development and interactions.

Bolting—Dramatic stem elongation in a rosette plant that normally precedes flowering.

Bud scales—A layer of protective scales that encase and protect buds.

Calyx—The lowermost or outermost floral whorl; collectively called sepals.

Carpel—A part of the innermost floral whorl. Each carpel contains one or more ovules.

Cell cycle—The activity within the nucleus from one nuclear division to the next.

Chromoprotein—A pigment consisting of a protein with an attached chromophore.

Chromophore—The chemical group that is responsible for absorbing light.

Circadian rhythm—A rhythm with a periodicity of approximately 24 hours.

Climacteric—A sudden rise in respiratory rate in fruits associated with the evolution of ethylene and ripening.

Coleoptile—The protective sheath that surrounds the meristem and first leaf of a grass embryo.

Cork cambium—The secondary meristem that produces the cork or outer bark of a woody stem or root.

Corolla—The petals of a flower.

Corpus—A body of cells that divide in various planes and contribute to the bulk of the shoot.

Cortex—The region of a young stem or root between the epidermis and the vascular cylinder; used primarily for storage.

Cotyledon—The seed leaf; a nutrient storage organ in dicots and a nutrient absorptive structure in monocots.

Critical day length—The length of photoperiod that determines whether or not long and short day plants will flower.

Glossary

Critical photoperiod—The duration of light exposure that influences plant flowering behavior and determines whether a plant is a long-day plant or a short-day plant.

Cross-pollination—The transfer of pollen between flowers on different plants.

Cryogenic storage—Storage at extremely cold temperatures, usually in liquid nitrogen (-196° C).

Cryoprotective proteins—Proteins that protect membranes and macro-molecules from ice crystal damage in the protoplast.

Cuticle—A waxy layer on the outer surface of the epidermis.

Cyclin—A small protein involved in determining progression through the cell cycle.

Cyclin-dependent kinase, or **CDK**—An enzyme that is activated by cyclin and that initiates the onset of the S and M phases in the cell cycle.

Cytokinin—A plant hormone whose primary function is to promote cell division.

Day-neutral plants—Plants that flower irrespective of photoperiod.

De-etiolation—The reversal of etiolation, usually promoted by phytochrome.

Dicotyledons—A class of angiosperms characterized by having two cotyledons.

Diurnal rhythm—A rhythm reflecting a process that is active only during the day; for example, photosynthesis. (Opposite of nocturnal).

Dormancy—A failure of seeds and buds to grow until special conditions are met.

Double fertilization—A unique characteristic of angiosperms in which the egg nucleus is fertilized by one sperm nucleus to form the zygote and the polar nuclei are fertilized by the second sperm nucleus to produce the endosperm.

Embryo—The immature plant in a seed.

Embryo sac—The female reproductive structure prior to fertilization.

Endogenous—Internal.

Endosperm—A seed tissue that provides nutrients for the developing embryo and germinating seed.

Entrainment—The process of synchronizing a circadian rhythm to an external cycle.

Epidermis—The outermost cell layers of leaves, young stems, and other organs.

Epigeal (Gk. *epi*, above; *geo*, earth)—A pattern of germination in which the cotyledons are lifted above the soil line.

Ethylene—A plant hormone involved primarily in the ripening of fruit.

Etiolated—The condition of a seedling in the absence of light; characterized by increased stem elongation, poor leaf expansion, and white or yellow color due to the absence of chlorophyll.

Exine—The outer wall of a pollen grain.

Expansin—An enzyme that loosens cross-linked cellulose molecules in the cell and thus allows cell expansion.

Floral-identity genes—A set of genes that programs the apex to change from the production of leaf primordia to the production of floral primordia.

Florigen—A hypothetical plant hormone that promotes flowering.

Flowering-time genes—A set of genes that determines when the meristem is susceptible to the floral stimulus.

Fluence rate—A measure of the amount of light falling on an object.

Free-running period—The inherent periodicity of a rhythmic phenomenon; not influenced by external factors.

Freezing-tolerance—The capacity of a plant to withstand freezing temperatures without injury.

Germination—The resumption of embryo growth in an otherwise quiescent seed.

Gibberellins—A group of plant hormones primarily noted for controlling the growth of intact stems.

Glycans—Small carbohydrate molecules that form cross-links with cellulose microfibrils in the plant cell wall.

Glossary

Gravitropism—A growth response to the force of gravity.

Gymnosperm—A seed plant such as the conifers whose seeds are not enclosed within an ovary.

Gynoecium—Collectively, the carpels or female reproductive structures in the pistil of an angiosperm flower.

Hormone—A chemical produced by the plant in small quantities that carries messages between cells.

Hydrophilic—Having an affinity for water; water-loving.

Hypocotyl (*hypo*: Gk. under or less than)—Section of the stem in an embryo or young seedling that lies below the cotyledons and above the radicle.

Hypogeal (Gk. *hypo*, under; *geo*, earth)—A pattern of germination in which the coltyledons remain in the soil.

Imbibition—(L. *imbibere*, to drink in) The absorption of water by dry materials, such as seeds, wood, etc.

Imperfect flower—A flower lacking pistils or stamens.

Indole-3-acetic acid (**IAA**)—The most common naturally occurring auxin hormone.

Inferior ovary—The condition of an ovary when the sepals and petals appear to arise from its top.

Integuments—The tissue that encompasses the embryo sac. The integuments become the seed coat.

Kinetin—A synthetic cytokinin. The first cytokinin to be discovered, kinetin was manufactured from herring sperm DNA.

Lignin—A complex polymer that is deposited in the secondary cell wall and gives wood many of its characteristic properties.

Long-day plants—Plants that flower in response to a day-length longer than some critical value.

Lunar rhythm—An endogenous rhythm with a periodicity of approximately 28 days.

Megaspore mother cell—A diploid cell that divides by meiosis to give rise to the egg and other cells of the embryo sac.

Meristem (Gk. *merizein*, to divide)–A region of active cell division that gives rise to new plant tissues.

Mesocotyl—A region of the monocot embryonic axis that elongates to push the coleoptile and its enclosed leaf through the soil.

Mesophile—An organism that thrives best at moderate temperatures.

Microspore mother cell—A diploid cell in the anther that divides by meiosis to produce haploid pollen.

Monocotyledons—A class of angiosperms characterized by a single cotyledon or scutellum in the embryo.

Nyctiperiodism—(Gr. *nuktos*, night) The inverse of photoperiodism, with the emphasis on the length of the dark period.

Nyctinastic movements—The periodic rise and fall of leaves. Also known as sleep movements.

Organ-identity genes—A set of genes that determines the sequence and form of floral appendages.

Osmosis—The net diffusion of water across a differentially permeable, or cellular, membrane in response to the concentration or chemical potential of water.

Ovary—The enlarged basal portion of the pistil.

Parthenocarpy—The development of a fruit in the absence of pollination or fertilization. Parthenocarpy can be stimulated by the application of auxin. The resulting fruit is seedless.

Pedicel—The stalk that supports a flower.

Peduncle—The stalk that supports a single flower.

Perfect flower—A flower that has functional pistils and stamens.

Pericarp (Gk. *peri*, around + *karpos*, fruit)—The mature ovary wall or fruit wall.

Pericycle—A ring of cells that gives rise to secondary roots.

Period—The time required for a plant to complete a single cycle.

Petals—The floral appendage that is usually brightly colored.

Glossary

Phloem—The portion of the vascular tissue responsible for conducting organic solutes.

Phosphorylation—A reaction in which a phosphate group is added to another molecule, such as ADP or protein.

Photomorphogenesis—Light-dependent changes in plant form or function.

Photon—A particle of light energy.

Photoperiod—Day length.

Photoperiodism—A response to the duration and timing of light and dark periods.

Photoreversible—A reaction that is driven forward and in reverse by light.

Phototropin—A chromoprotein pigment that absorbs the light responsible for driving phototropism.

Phototropism—A growth response that is determined by a light gradient.

Phytochrome—The photoreceptor for red, far-red photoreversible responses.

Pistil—The central, female reproductive structure of a flower, consisting of a stigma, style, and ovary.

Plumule—The apical bud of an embryo.

Polar transport—Unidirectional transport, especially of auxin, which is synthesized at the apex of a stem and transported toward the base.

Pollination—The transfer of pollen from an anther to a stigma.

Primary cell wall—The first cell wall that is laid down in a growing cell.

Primary leaves—The leaves in an embryo that are the first to expand when the young seedling reaches the soil surface.

Primary tissues—Tissues that are derived from apical meristems.

Primordium, *pl.* **primordia** —An organ in its earliest stage of formation.

Protochlorophyll—A pigment similar to chlorophyll that accumulates in dark-grown tissue. Protochlorophyll is converted to chlorophyll in the light.

Psychrophiles—Organisms that best grow at low temperatures.

Pulvinus—A bulbous structure found at the base of leaves and petioles and that is the "motor" that drives sleep movements.

Quantum, *pl.* **quanta**—A particle of electromagnetic radiation. A quantum of light energy is a photon.

Quiescent—A term used to describe a seed that is not germinating but will germinate when provided with water and oxygen at physiological temperature.

Radicle—The embryonic root.

Receptacle—The top of a floral stem or peduncle that bears the floral appendages.

Riboflavin—A yellow pigment that is the chromophore for the phototropin molecule. Riboflavin has many other functions in plants and animal metabolism.

Root cap—A mass of cells that covers and protects the root apical meristem. The root cap is the principal organ for the detection of gravity by roots.

Scarification—Any process that breaks, scratches, mechanically alters, or softens the seed coats to make them permeable to water and oxygen.

Scutellum—The single cotyledon in seeds of monocots, especially of corn and the cereal grains. Its principal function is to absorb nutrients from the endosperm and transfer them to the embryo.

Secondary growth—Growth resulting from the activities of secondary meristems such as the vascular cambium.

Secondary tissues—Tissues laid down by the vascular cambium.

Secondary wall—The wall that forms after a cell has enlarged to its maximum size. The secondary wall is laid down on the inside of the primary cell wall.

Seed bank—The population of non-germinated seeds in the soil. Seeds are available to germinate when the soil is disturbed.

Seed coat—The outer protective layer of a seed.

Self-incompatibility—The inability of pollen to fertilize ovules in the same flower due to chemicals and other factors.

Glossary

Sepal—One of the lowermost whorl of floral appendages. Sepals cover the floral bud before it opens. Sepals are often inconspicuous but may be brightly colored like the petals.

Short-day plants—Plants that flower in response to day-length less than some critical photoperiod.

Simple fruits—A fruit derived from a single carpel or several united carpels.

Spectral composition—The balance of wavelengths in a light source or a beam of light. Also known as light quality or spectral energy distribution.

Spectral energy distribution—The color composition of visible light.

Statoliths (Gk. *statos*, stationary + *lithos*, stone)—Starch grains or other cytoplasmic inclusions that act as gravity sensors.

Stigma—The portion of the pistil that serves as a receptive surface for pollen and on which they germinate.

Stomata, *sg.* **stoma**—Pores in the surface of a leaf through which carbon dioxide, oxygen, and water vapor are exchanged between the leaf and the atmosphere.

Stratification—The technique of subjecting moistened cold-requiring seeds to an extended period of low temperature to force germination.

Style—The column of tissue between the stigma and the ovary through which the pollen tube grows.

Succulent plants—Plants with fleshy water-filled leaves or stems; native to dry habitats.

Superior ovary—An ovary that is above and free from the sepals and petals.

Target cells—Cells that are intended to be responsive to a particular hormone.

Thermonasty—A differential growth response that is due to temperature changes, such as the opening and closure of tulip petals.

Thermoperiodism—A growth response to periodic (e.g., day/night) fluctuations of temperature.

Thermophiles—Organisms that favor habitats characterized by high temperatures.

Tube nucleus—The nucleus that directs the pollen tube as it grows down through the style.

Tunica—The outermost layers of cells in a meristem.

Turgor—The condition characterized by a cell that is swollen or distended resulting from the osmotic flow of water into the cell.

Ultradian rhythms—Rhythms of metabolic activity within periods of minutes or hours.

Vascular cambium—A cylindrical sheath of meristematic cells around a stem or root; the vascular cambium produces secondary xylem and secondary phloem.

Vascular tissue—The water- and solute-conducting tissues that are unique to vascular plants.

Vernalization—The use of a cold treatment to alter flowering behavior.

Winter hardy—A species of plant capable of acclimating to low temperatures.

Xylem—The vascular tissue primarily responsible for conducting water and dissolve minerals.

Zeitgeber—A factor such as a light-on signal that synchronizes or entrains an endogenous rhythm with an external cycle.

Zygote—The diploid cell that results from the fusion of a haploid sperm nucleus with a haploid egg nucleus. Through cell division the zygote gives rise to the embryo.

Bibliography and Further Reading

General Biology and Botany

Alberts, B. et al. *Molecular Biology of the Cell*. Garland Publishing, 2002.

Attenborough, D. *The Private Life of Plants: A Natural History of Plant Behavior*. Princeton: Princeton University Press, 1995.

Campbell, N. A., J. B. Reece. *Biology*. 6th ed. Benjamin Cummings, 2001.

Galston, A.W. *Life Processes of Plants*. New York: Scientific American Library, 1994.

Hartman, H. T., W. J. Flocker, A. M. Kofranek. *Plant Science. Growth, Development, and Utilization of Cultivated Plants*. Englewood Cliffs, NJ: Prentice Hall, 1981.

Hopkins, W. G., N. P. A. Hüner. *Introduction to Plant Physiology*, 3rd ed. New York: John Wiley & Sons, 2004.

King, J. *Reaching for the Sun: How Plants Work*. Cambridge: Cambridge University Press, 1997.

Raven, P. H., R. F. Evert, S. E. Eichhorn. *Biology of Plants*. New York: Worth Publishers, 1999.

Wilkins, M. *Plant Watching*. New York: Facts on File, 1988.

Flowers

Greyson, R. I. *The Development of Flowers*. New York: Oxford University Press, 1994.

Hormones

Davies, P. J. *Plant Hormones: Physiology, Biochemistry, and Molecular Biology*. Boston: Kluwer Academic Publishers, 1995.

Photoperiodism and Biological Clocks

Colasanti, J., V. Sundareson. Florigen Enters the Molecular Age: Long-distance Signals that Cause Plants to Flower. *Trends in Biochemical Science* 25 (2000): 236-240.

Konc, T., M. Ishiura. The Circadian Clocks of Plants and Cyanobacteria. *Trends in Plant Science*. 4 (1999): 171-176.

Sweeney, B. *Rhythmic Phenomena in Plants*. San Diego: Academic Press, 1987.

Thomas, B., D. Vince-Prue. *Photoperiodism in Plants*. San Diego: Academic Press, 1997.

Phytochrome

Kendrick, R. F., B. Frankland. *Phytochrome and Plant Growth.* Edward Arnold, 1983.

Sage, L. *Pigment of the Imagination: A History of Phytochrome Research.* San Diego: Academic Press, 1992.

Seeds

Bewley, J. D., M. Black. *Seeds: Physiology of Development and Germination.* New York: Plenum Press, 1994.

Turner, C. B. *Seed Sowing and Saving: Step-by-Step Techniques for Collecting Seeds.* Pownal, Vermont: Storey Communications, 1998.

Websites

Online Botany Textbook

http://www.biologie.uni.hamburg.de/b-online/e00/contents.htm
   (or access as Botany Online through Google)

http://www.extension.oregonstate.edu/mg/botany/index.html

Online Biology Textbook

http://users.rcn.com/jkimball.ma.ultranet/BiologyPages/

Giant pumpkins

http://www.backyardgardener.com/record.html

http://www.pumpkinnook.com/giants/record.htm

http://www.howarddill.com

Gravitropism

http://plantsinmotion.bio.indiana.edu/plantmotion/starthere.html

Winter Cereals

http://www.usask.ca/agriculture/plantsci/winter_cereals/#topten

http://www.ku.edu/carrie/texts/carrie_books/malin/

Index

Index

Picture Credits

William G. Hopkins received a B.A. in biology from Wesleyan University and a Ph.D. in botany from Indiana University. His postdoctoral training was conducted at Brookhaven National Laboratories. He has taught at Bryn Mawr College and the University of Western Ontario, where he is now Professor Emeritus of biology. Dr. Hopkins has taught primarily in the areas of plant physiology and cell biology, was responsible for design and implementation of an honors program in cell biology, and served many years as an undergraduate counselor. In 1988, Dr. Hopkins was awarded the university's Gold Medal for Excellence in Teaching. He has served in numerous administrative posts, including several years as Chair of the university's Academic Review Board. His research and publications have focused on the role of light and temperature in plant development, the organization of chlorophyll-protein complexes, and energy transformations in chloroplasts. Dr. Hopkins has been a contributing author to two high school biology textbooks and is the senior author of *Introduction to Plant Physiology*.